Diane Warner's

Contemporary Guide to

WEDDING CEREMONIES

Hundreds of Creative Personal Touches and Tips for a Wedding to Remember

 A division of The Career Press, Inc.
Franklin Lakes, NJ

DIANE WARNER'S CONTEMPORARY GUIDE TO WEDDING ETIQUETTE
EDITED AND TYPESET BY KATE HENCHES
Cover design by DesignConcept
Printed in the U.S.A. by Book-mart Press

To order this title, please call toll-free 1-800-CAREER-1 (NJ and Canada: 201-848-0310) to order using VISA or MasterCard, or for further information on books from Career Press.

The Career Press, Inc., 3 Tice Road, PO Box 687,
Franklin Lakes, NJ 07417
www.careerpress.com
www.newpagebooks.com

Library of Congress Cataloging-in-Publication Data

Warner, Diane.
    Diane Warner's contemporary guide to wedding etiquette : advice from America's most trusted wedding expert / by Diane Warner.
        p. cm.
    Includes index.
    ISBN 1-56414-761-4 (pbk.)
        1. Wedding etiquette. I. Title.

BJ2051.W265 2005
395.2′2--dc22

                                                                2004048620

DEDICATION

I dedicate this book to my husband, Jack.
Thank you for your patience, encouragement,
and support through the years.

ACKNOWLEDGMENTS

I would like to thank Michael Pye, Senior Acquisitions Editor at New Page Books, along with Kristen Parkes, Kate Henches, Gina Talucci, and all members of the editorial staff who helped me put this book together.

A big thank-you to all the brides, grooms, and wedding service providers who so generously shared unique qualities of their wedding ceremonies, or the ceremonies they helped plan.

Finally, thanks to Jeff Herman, my literary agent.

CONTENTS

INTRODUCTION

Your wedding day is the most significant, life-changing milestone of your life. On this day you will put your past behind you. No longer will you be a single person enjoying the single life, with its singular, often spontaneous, pleasures, but you'll be a married person, sharing your pleasures and concerns with someone else. This isn't just another party, but the most important day of your life.

A wedding is time-consuming to plan. In fact, it is said that it takes more than 700 hours to put it all together, from the rehearsal dinner, to the ceremony, the reception, and the great getaway to your honeymoon destination. A wedding is also an expensive affair, averaging more than $25,000 nationwide, so plan it carefully with thought and care. You'll remember this day for the rest of your lives.

Your wedding day is also the day when you publicly commit yourselves to each other in marriage, not only as you recite your vows, but as you participate in all the special elements you decide to include. For example, you may decide to add handfasting, the lighting of a unity candle, or a ceremony of wishing stones. Or, if you have children from a previous marriage, you may want to include them in your vows, or with a Circle of Acceptance or a Family Medal-lion Ceremony.

The important thing is this: personalize your wedding ceremony as much as you possibly can. Don't accept a cookie-cutter wedding, with all its predictable elements. Modify, add, or delete until your ceremony is uniquely yours. In doing so, it will be personal and special, not only demonstrating your sacred commitment to each other, establishing a foundation for a lasting marriage, but also inspiring your guests to rejoice and share your commitment.

In this book you'll find hundreds of ways to personalize your ceremony, beginning with the big questions: choosing your ceremony venue, members of your wedding party, and a wedding planner, if you decide to use one. You'll also learn how to personalize your venue by choosing a theme and creating an ambience.

Most of this book, however, is devoted to the elements of the ceremony itself, including conventional elements, such as the invocation, vows, pronouncement and bene-diction, and a myriad of optional and special elements, such as readings, covenant of salt, jumping the broom, or a dove release.

Also included are examples of religious and secular cer-emonies. You'll find examples of Jewish, Catholic, Protes-tant, and Interfaith ceremonies, along with other popular choices, such as the Civil Ceremony, Encore Ceremony, New Life Ceremony, and Nature Ceremony.

Enjoy your journey as you plan your special day. Take it slow and give your ceremony a lot of thought—it isn't to be taken lightly. And remember, when you look back on your ceremony in the years to come, it should be a touching, poignant memory. You'll be glad you took the time to personalize it.

I.

EARLY CEREMONY QUESTIONS

Where do you start? You're still basking in the glow of your recent engagement, and the work involved in planning your ceremony may seem daunting. It can indeed be daunting, and even overwhelming, which is why most couples accept whatever their officiant suggests, including traditional order of service, wording of the vows, and other conventional elements—just what everyone expects to see at any wedding ceremony.

Because you purchased this book, I suspect you're not willing to accept a cookie-cutter ceremony—you want your wedding to be unique and personal. So, take it in little bites; don't plan it all in one day. Look at all the options before deciding on anything.

The first place to start is by answering these early questions:

- ∞ How do we choose our ceremony venue and officiant?
- ∞ How do we choose the members of our wedding party?

∞   Should we hire a wedding planner to help us?

The three chapters included in this section will help you with these decisions so that you'll have a foundation on which to build the rest of your ceremony choices.

Chapter 1

YOUR CEREMONY VENUE AND OFFICIANT

Where would you like to get married? Will your wedding be formal or informal? Indoor or outdoor? Religious or secular? Do you want your ceremony and reception at the same site? Who do you want to officiate at your wedding?

Most weddings take place in a religious venue, such as a church, chapel, temple, or cathedral. However, you may have a religious ceremony that takes place outside a religious venue. For instance, your family pastor might marry you in a private home or in your grandparents' rose garden.

Popular Ceremony Venues

In addition to traditional religious venues, 21st-century brides and grooms are choosing unique venues for their weddings. You can locate these venues through word-of-mouth, in the Yellow Pages, by calling government offices, or through your local chamber of commerce or historical society.

Here are popular venues:

- Private home
- Private club
- Hotel ballroom

- Resort
- Golf course
- Garden
- Restaurant
- Beside a river, lake, or waterfall
- Seashore
- Community clubhouse
- Elk's hall, or similar
- Country inn
- Rented tent
- National, state, or city park
- Houseboat
- Museum
- Art gallery
- Senior center
- Historical site
- Mansion
- Theater
- Schoolhouse
- College campus
- Courthouse grounds
- Marina
- Private wedding chapel
- Yacht
- Arboretum
- Private campgrounds
- Docked ferry

Questions to Ask Before Renting a Venue

Once you've found a suitable venue for your ceremony, ask a lot of questions before signing an agreement or contract. Here are suggested questions you may want to ask:

- Will the venue be available on the date/time of your ceremony?
- What is the legal occupancy allowed for the venue?
- Are any other weddings scheduled for the same day?
- What is the rental fee for the venue? How many hours does this include? Does it allow time for decorating and undecorating? Is it available for the wedding rehearsal? If so, is this fee included, or is it extra?
- Are there any other extra or unexpected fees that may be charged? If so, what are they?
- How are fees to be paid? A deposit now? The balance when?
- Do you provide such things as an aisle runner, silk flower arrangements, candles, kneeling bench, and so on?
- Do you furnish a lighting technician, wedding coordinator, janitorial services, musicians, and so on?
- If so, are there additional fees for these services?
- Are there any restrictions regarding the decorations, such as attaching floral bouquets at the end of each pew or aisle? To the walls? To candle sconces?

- ∞ If it's a religious venue, are there any restrictions regarding musical selections, modesty of wedding attire, flash photography, readings, poems, use of lighted candles, age of flower girls or ring bearers, and so on?

- ∞ If it's a religious venue, are there also restrictions as to who may officiate? Are we obligated to use the venue's clergyman, rabbi, or priest? Or, may we have our pastor or a civil officiant marry us?

- ∞ Are there any restrictions on tossing items (rice, petals, bird seed)?

- ∞ What type of guest parking is available?

- ∞ Are there bride and groom dressing rooms?

- ∞ Does the venue have wheelchair accessibility?

- ∞ Does the venue offer outdoor facilities?

Note: Never place a deposit on a ceremony venue until you know for sure the date and time are acceptable to your officiant, members of your wedding party, primary vendors, and close friends and relatives.

Who Do You Want to Officiate at Your Ceremony?

This is an important question that may determine your selection of a ceremony venue. For example, if you want your family's Methodist minister to officiate your wedding at a Nazarene church in another town, will that be acceptable to the minister and the church? Or, does the religious venue require that you use their clergy to perform the ceremony? Or, will the venue allow your personal pastor to co-officiate with the venue's clergy?

If you have your heart set on having a certain person marry you, you need to start there first. Once that is settled, these are questions you should ask:

- Is that person available to officiate on the date and time of your wedding?

- Is the officiant willing to travel to your ceremony site? This is an especially important question if you're planning on a civil ceremony performed by a judge, justice of the peace, or other licensed state officiant.

- Will the officiant be available for your rehearsal and rehearsal dinner?

- What documents should you bring to your first meeting with this officiant?

- When should the marriage license be delivered to the officiant?

- Will pre-marital counseling be required? If so, how many sessions?

- Does the officiant have any restrictions regarding divorced persons, if applicable?

- Will your officiant allow you to personalize the ceremony? Vows? Readings? Choice of music? Type of sermon or message your officiant will deliver, if any?

- What will your officiant wear? If you are planning a costume-style wedding, such as renaissance, Victorian, country-western, and so on, will the officiant be open to wearing costume-styled attire?

- What is the officiant's fee? Are there additional fees for attending the wedding rehearsal or traveling to the ceremony venue?

As you can see, it's important to coordinate your officiant and ceremony venue to be sure they are compatible. That's the reason why you should not reserve one or the other before you're sure they will work together.

Take your time as you make these decisions. You'll be glad you did.

Chapter 2

MEMBERS OF YOUR WEDDING PARTY

One of the most exciting aspects of planning your wedding is selecting the members of your wedding party. You'll need to choose these important participants as soon as possible after announcing your engagement. However, don't make these selections until you've given them a lot of thought. A common mistake, for example, is when the bride asks her best friend to be her maid of honor, but later realizes she really should have asked her sister to fulfill this role. The key is to tread lightly as you compose your list.

Following are those you may want to include in your wedding party, considerations you should make before deciding, and what will be expected from each of them.

Attendants

Attendants include maid/matron of honor, best man, groomsmen, bridesmaids, flower girl, and ring bearer. Here are questions to consider when making your list:

- How many attendants would you like to have? You'll need to take into account the location and formality of your wedding. If you're having a small, informal wedding on the back

patio of your parents' home, it may be silly to
have 14 bridesmaids and 14 groomsmen. However, if you're planning a large, elegant wedding at the biggest cathedral in town, you may
have as many attendants as you would like.

Note: It is no longer necessary to keep the numbers
equal when it comes to the bride's and groom's attendants.

∞ Does your ceremony venue have any religious
restrictions regarding honor attendants?

If your ceremony will take place in a house of
worship, check with your officiant to see if
there are any religious restrictions regarding
your maid/matron of honor and best man.
Some faiths require that your official witnesses
(aka your honor attendants) be members of
your faith, and they may be required to attend
special pre-wedding classes before they'll be
allowed to participate in the ceremony.

∞ Who is your closest, dearest friend?

You may choose your best friend, your closest
relative, or the bride may choose her closest
male friend or the groom may choose his
favorite female friend, to be their honor attendants. It's common these days for the bride
to have a man of honor instead of a maid/
matron of honor, and the groom to have a best
woman instead of a best man.

Note: A popular trend today is for the bride to ask her
mother to serve as her honor attendant and the groom to
ask his father to serve as his best man.

⚭ What about your siblings and your fiancé's siblings?

If at all possible, include all the siblings in your wedding party, whether as the bride's attendants or the groom's attendants.

⚭ What about other close friends?

If you come up with a list of a dozen close friends, in addition to your honor attendants and siblings, you may have more candidates than vacancies on your list of attendants. If so, include several of them in other ways, such as guest book hostess, reception host, candlelighters, or they may perform a musical selection or deliver a reading during your ceremony.

⚭ Which friends have asked you to serve as an attendant at their weddings?

You should give consideration to any friends who fall into this category, but be aware that you are not obligated to ask these friends to be your attendants.

Note: It's become trendy to designate "honorary attendants." These are attendants who are very close to you and would have been in your wedding party if they could. For example, in the case of the groom's brother who's serving in Iraq and can't come home for the wedding, he may be mentioned in the ceremony program with this suggested wording:

Honorary best man: Clinton Webster Jones, the groom's brother, currently serving in the U.S. Army, stationed in Iraq.

Responsibilities of the Bride's Honor Attendant

The bride's maid or matron of honor is the person the bride counts on to help her during the weeks preceding the wedding, and to serve as her personal assistant on her wedding day. Here are her duties:

- Helps address invitations, runs errands, makes telephone calls, and keeps a record of gifts received.
- Helps the bride shop for her gown, bridal accessories, and the bridesmaids' attire.
- Along with the bridesmaids, she plans and hosts the bridal luncheon (unless this luncheon is hosted by the bride).
- Arranges final fittings for the bride's and bridesmaids' gowns.
- Helps the bride pack for her honeymoon.
- Along with the bridesmaids, she shops for a joint wedding gift.
- Helps the bride dress before the ceremony.
- Precedes the bride down the aisle.
- Holds the bride's bouquet during the ceremony.
- Adjusts the bride's veil and train after she arrives at the altar.
- Safeguards the groom's wedding ring until the ring ceremony.
- Signs the wedding certificate.
- Stands in the receiving line, if asked.
- Dances with the best man during the reception.
- Helps the bride change into her going-away outfit.

Responsibilities of the Bridesmaids

The bridesmaids have fewer duties:

- ∞ Help the honor attendant plan and host the bridal shower.

- ∞ Run small errands and makes telephone calls, if asked.

- ∞ Help plan the bridal luncheon, unless the bride hosts it.

- ∞ Stand in the receiving line, if asked.

- ∞ Smile, look pretty, and dance with the groom's attendants during the reception.

Responsibilities of the Best Man

The best man has many important responsibilities, including:

- ∞ Helps the groom locate an acceptable tuxedo rental store and arranges for the groomsmen to be measured for their tuxedos.

- ∞ Picks up the tuxedos and transports them to the location the men will dress for the ceremony.

- ∞ Confirms and/or picks up anything the groom has ordered, such as the bride's wedding ring that was being sized at the jewelers, or the airline tickets and travel itineraries from the travel agent.

- ∞ Plans and organizes the bachelor party.

- ∞ On the wedding day, he makes sure the groom has everything he needs for the honeymoon, including medications, passport, hotel or rental-car confirmations, ATM cards, money, keys, and so forth.

- ⌀ Safeguards the marriage license and sees that it is delivered to the officiant before the ceremony. He also signs this document after the ceremony.
- ⌀ Helps the groom and the groomsmen dress for the ceremony.
- ⌀ Safeguards the bride's wedding ring until the ring ceremony.
- ⌀ Delivers the fee to the officiant.
- ⌀ Stands in the receiving line, if asked.
- ⌀ Dances with the bride, her mother, and all the bridal attendants.
- ⌀ Offers the first toast to the bride and groom during the reception.
- ⌀ Helps the groom change into his going-away clothes.
- ⌀ Sees that the couple's luggage is placed in their getaway vehicle.

Responsibilities of the Groomsmen / Ushers

The groom's attendants, aka groomsmen, often serve double duty as ushers. If they don't serve double duty, the groom will need to choose ushers. Here are their duties:

- ⌀ Help decorate the getaway vehicle.
- ⌀ Help seat the wedding guests, hand out programs, if provided, and roll out the aisle runner, if one is planned. The groomsmen (or ushers) offer their right arms as they escort women down the aisle. If a woman is accompanied by a man, the man follows behind the woman. If a guest hands an usher or groomsmen a pew card, the guest is seated according to the directions on the card. If not, the guest

is asked whether he or she is a guest of the bride or groom. The bride's guests are seated on the left and the groom's on the right for a Christian or Catholic ceremony. The reverse is true for a Jewish ceremony.

∞ Smile, look handsome, and dance with the bride, both mothers, and every bridesmaid during the reception.

Flower Girl

Your flower girl has only one responsibility:

∞ Precedes the bride down the aisle, carrying a basket of flowers or tossing rose petals in the bride's path. She may walk beside the ring bearer.

Note: If you have more than one candidate for this position, in order to prevent hurt feelings, include two or more flower girls.

Ring Bearer

Your ring bearer has only one responsibility:

∞ Precedes the flower girl down the aisle, as he carries the bride's ring on a silver tray or attached with a ribbon to a satin pillow (usually a fake ring because the real ring is safeguarded by the best man).

Note: If there is no flower girl, the ring bearer immediately precedes the bride down the aisle. The same rule applies for the flower girl: If you have more than one candidate for this position, you may have two ring bearers walk side by side down the aisle. One of the ring bearers carries the bride's "ring" and the other the groom's "ring."

Trainbearers or Pages

If the bride's gown has a long train, you may have a trainbearer or page carry the train. A trainbearer is a little girl and a page is a little boy. If your train is extra full or long, you may have two trainbearers, two pages, or one trainbearer and one page. This is an excellent way to include children in your ceremony who weren't able to serve as flower girl or ring bearer. This child or children have only one responsibility:

- Carry the bridal gown's train during the processional and recessional.

Junior Attendants

Junior attendants are usually between 8 and 15 years of age. Again, this is an excellent way to include younger girls and boys in your ceremony.

They have very easy duty:

- The bride's junior attendants are called junior bridesmaids and precede the bridesmaids down the aisle. They stand next to, or at the end of, the row of bridesmaids.
- The groom's junior attendants are called junior groomsmen or ushers and stand next to, or at the end of, the row of groomsmen.

Candle-lighters

Candle-lighters may be teenage girls or boys. Here are their responsibilities:

- Light the candles during the candle-lighting prelude, which immediately precedes the seating of the bride's mother. They enter from the rear of the ceremony venue, slowly lighting the candles that have been arranged around the site, such as on sconces mounted on pillars or on candelabra stands in front of the venue.

⬭ Snuff out the candles after the recessional, during the musical postlude.

Bell-ringers

Bell-ringers are boys or girls of any age who carry crystal or brass bells. They have one responsibility:

⬭ Walk up and down the aisles of the ceremony venue, ringing their bells to let the guests know the ceremony is about to begin.

As you can see by this long list, you can include many people of all ages in your wedding party. Don't angst over which little girl to serve as your flower girl. If you have three sisters, each with a 5-year-old girl, use all three. What could be cuter than three little girls tossing rose petals in your path? In other words, try to work in everyone who is important in your life.

Chapter 3

WEDDING PLANNER

A wedding planner, sometimes known as a bridal consultant, wedding consultant, wedding director, wedding professional, or a wedding coordinator, can relieve much of the stress in planning a wedding.

Types of Wedding Planners

You'll find quite an array of wedding planners, including:

- ∞ The wedding consultant provided by a church, synagogue, or secular venue. It is the duty of one of these consultants to help you plan a wedding acceptable to policies set by the venue. For example, if you decide to get married in your local church, you may be required to enlist, and pay for, the services of such a coordinator. The expense for this type of limited service is usually quite affordable.

- ∞ A department store employee working as a bridal consultant. This type of consultant is usually limited to bridal and wedding party attire and may or may not be paid a commission by the department store.

- A professional wedding planner who helps plan and coordinate all or part of the wedding, often in conjunction with wedding vendors. Their fees vary from a flat fee to an hourly fee to a percentage of the wedding expenses.

- A wedding-day planner who works with you to see that the plans you have already made on your own are carried out during the rehearsal and the day of the wedding itself. This type of planner may charge a flat fee or hourly fee.

Services Provided by a Full-Service Wedding Planner

A full-service professional provides many services. Here are a few:

- Helps you select your ceremony and reception venues.

- Helps you choose a theme for your wedding.

- Helps you choose wedding attire, decorations, music, and other elements that coordinate with your wedding theme.

- Helps you choose vendors and service providers, including a florist, catering service, musicians, photographer, videographer, and so on.

- Ensures communication between you, the members of your wedding party, the ceremony and reception personnel, and all the vendors and service providers. For example, your florist should have a photograph of your bridal gown before designing your bridal bouquet.

- Serves as your financial advisor, counselor, etiquette expert, referee, and friend.

    ∽ Sees that your dreams come true and your rehearsal and wedding day run smoothly.

Note: One of these professionals is a must if you're planning a long distance wedding, or, as with so many career women, you're already on overload at work and don't have time to plan a large wedding.

How to Find a Reputable Wedding Planner

Many people call themselves professional wedding planners, although they may have very little training and experience. What you need, however, is a professional who is trained, certificated, and a member of a national association, such as:

    ∽ Association of Bridal Consultants
        (*www.bridalassn.com*)

    ∽ June Wedding, Inc. (*www.junewedding.com*)

    ∽ Weddings Beautiful Worldwide
        (*www.weddingsbeautiful.com*)

You can locate one of these professionals by asking around, by checking your local yellow pages, or by accessing their Websites.

II.

PERSONALIZE YOUR CEREMONY VENUE

It was a big decision, but you've finally chosen your ceremony venue. If you're planning a religious ceremony, it will probably be a church or synagogue, although, depending on your religious faith, a religious ceremony may take place at a secular location as well. Or, you may have chosen a unique venue, such as a historic castle for a Renaissance ceremony, or a lakefront beach for a nature ceremony. Whatever your venue, however, you want it to have a personalized theme and ambience.

The chapters included in this section offer a myriad of ways to pull this off. Chapter 4 suggests ceremony themes for you to consider, and Chapter 5 gives helpful advice for creating ambience.

This is going to be fun for you, as you begin to give your ceremony a special personality.

CEREMONY THEME

You need a theme for your ceremony, whether simple or complex. Your theme may follow the natural ambience of your ceremony site, such as a beach or a garden. Or you may follow your family's ethnic or cultural tradition, such as a Swedish theme with soft yellows and eggshell blues. You may also, however, choose one of the popular ceremony themes for today's weddings, such as Victorian or Black and White.

Following are themes for you to consider for your ceremony venue:

Victorian

A Victorian theme is nostalgic, romantic, and sentimental, with an abundance of lace, ribbons, hearts, and trailing ribbons. The bride and her attendants may wear Victorian style gowns, including bustled skirts and high buttoned shoes. The bridesmaids may also carry lace parasols.

The bride may carry a tussy mussy bouquet (a small cluster of flowers tied with ribbon, or inserted into an elegant cone-shaped silver holder). Lace is incorporated into the bridesmaids' bouquets and floral decorations.

Home

A home wedding provides its own theme: charm, nostalgia, intimacy. The first step is to unclutter the rooms. Remove a few of the oversized pieces of furniture and clear away at least half of the knickknacks, family photos, and so on. This will leave room for rented white folding chairs and a few floral arrangements. The fireplace mantle can be decorated with greens, flowers, candles, and ribbons. An altar can be assembled quite easily by covering any small table with a lace or damask tablecloth. If you would like to have a kneeling bench, you may be able to borrow or rent one.

You may also choose an indoor garden theme for your home wedding, which is explained below.

Indoor Garden

Any indoor venue, including a home or a church, can be converted into an indoor garden. Consider using wrought iron benches, trellises, white wooden arbors, and picket fencing. Then add colorful flowering potted plants, shrubs, and trees, whether fresh or silk.

Snowball

This is a wedding where everyone wears white, including the mothers and grandmothers. The ribbons, flowers, and any other decorations are also white. The trick is for all the whites to be the same shade of white. Start with the most important purchase: the bride's gown. Then, take a sample of the gown's fabric with you whenever you're shopping for ribbons, bridesmaids' gowns, mothers' and grandmothers' gowns, flowers, and so on.

A snowball wedding is beautiful and romantic.

Christmas

A Christmas wedding can be any wedding that takes place during the month of December. This is an easy theme to work with because of the Christmas trees, holly, poinsettias, candles, and evergreenery available during this month. Also, trail strands of tiny white Christmas tree lights over and around the decorations for a special touch of winter wonderland.

Black and White

All the wedding costumes are black and white. The men may wear black tuxedoes, the bridal attendants black gowns, the flower girl wears white, and the ring bearer wears black. This is a popular theme, but be careful to splash a little color around the venue, in the ribbons or flowers, or the wedding may lose its festive feeling of celebration.

Wreaths

Decorated wreaths can be used as pew decorations and bridesmaids' "bouquets." They may also be hung over candle sconces or candelabra. Large wreaths may be hung on the walls in the front of the venue.

Rose Garden

If your ceremony will be held in someone's backyard, in a park, or an existing garden, you can give the site a rose garden theme. The first step is to decide on a color, such as pink or yellow. The color you choose should coordinate with the bridesmaids' gowns, flower girl's dress, and any ribbons used in the decorations. Buy or borrow potted rose plants, along with as many fresh-cut roses as possible. Add fresh or silk green plants and trees, plus bird baths, and wrought iron benches.

If you come up short on fresh roses, fill in the gaps with silk roses in the same color.

Hearts and Flowers / Valentine's Day

A hearts and flowers theme is appropriate for any time of year, but especially for a Valentine wedding. This theme requires many decorated hearts of all sizes, and an abundance of fresh and potted flowers. Wrap the pots or floral containers with crepe paper and ribbons in the wedding colors. The hearts can be cut from cardboard or poster board, covered with crepe paper, and edged with paper or ribbon lace ruffles. Large hearts may be hung on each side at the front of the venue, and smaller hearts may be used to embellish the pew decorations, candle sconces, candelabra, and floral arrangements. Tiny hearts may also be attached to the ribbons that trail down from the bride's and bridesmaids' bouquets.

If the ceremony has an informal venue, you might also add heart shaped helium balloons tied to the backs of chairs, added to the floral arrangements, or placed in clusters elsewhere around the site.

Southern Antebellum

Round up white picket fences, a white arbor or gazebo, and as many fresh or silk magnolias, hydrangeas, or lilacs as you can find. The bride and her attendants may wear purchased or rented Southern-belle gowns with hoop skirts and parasols. The men can wear white dinner jackets with black ties, trousers, and pin-striped vests. If it's an evening wedding, decorate the site with white candles set in clear mason jars, plus tiny white Christmas lights.

Renaissance

Renaissance weddings are enormously popular these days. You should know, however, that one of these weddings is not only complicated to plan, but more expensive than an average wedding.

You can give any setting a Renaissance theme, however, some settings work best, such as a historic castle, beside an old covered bridge, on a farm, or in an open field.

Traditional Renaissance wedding attire is the most important element when creating this theme. The bride may wear a traditional ball gown with bell shaped sleeves, and her attendants may wear flowing gowns with pointy hats or flowered wreaths on their heads. The men usually wear velvet doublets, shirts with billowing sleeves, and feathered hats. The groom also wears a sword at his side.

For more ideas, attend a Renaissance festival or visit your local library to see back issues of *Renaissance Magazine*, or the Renaissance festival Website at *www.renaissancefestival.com)*.

Polynesian

This theme is a favorite among wedding guests because it reminds them of happy, carefree vacations spent in Hawaii. It works best around water, such as a swimming pool, a beach, or the banks of a lake or river.

Decorate your site with Tiki torches; conch shells; and colorful fresh, silk, or crepe paper flowers. The bride and groom may wear traditional Hawaiian wedding attire, the bridesmaids may wear colorful Hawaiian print gowns, and the groomsmen may wear white slacks and flowered Hawaiian shirts. Every member of the wedding party wears a fresh orchid lei, and every guest is presented with a silk orchid lei upon arrival.

Include the Hawaiian Wedding Song in your ceremony, plus any other Hawaiian favorites, especially during the prelude candle-lighting ceremony and the unity candle ceremony.

Country Western

This theme can be used for any informal venue, whether indoors or outdoors. The site is decorated with all things country western: lariats, cowboy hats, red bandanas, red checkered fabric, potted cacti, saddles, bales of hay, and, if you're lucky, perhaps you can find an old hay wagon.

Everyone dresses in western garb, including the bride, groom, all members of the wedding party, and the guests.

Other Themes

You can personalize your ceremony venue with any theme you like, whether it's been done before or not. For example, you and your fiancé may be totally into square dancing, or perhaps you're over-the-top NASCAR fans. Whatever your interests, you can incorporate them into your wedding theme.

Here are few ideas to whet your appetite:

- Autumn harvest
- Fourth of July
- Ice palace
- Romantic candlelight
- Love doves
- Celtic
- Mexican fiesta
- Oktoberfest
- Classic cars
- The 50s

- ∞ Halloween
- ∞ Beach party
- ∞ Gay 90s
- ∞ Tropical rain forest
- ∞ Cruiseship
- ∞ Ski resort
- ∞ Hollywood movie set
- ∞ Happy New Year

As you can see, the sky's the limit. So, depending on the formality of your wedding and ceremony venue, you have dozens of themes form which to choose.

Have fun!

Chapter 5

CEREMONY AMBIENCE

Every ceremony venue has a certain ambience, from "this-is-just-another-cookie-cutter-wedding" to "wow." If you want your ceremony venue to wow your guests, you'll need to create your own special ambience with flowers, decorations, lighting, and music.

Flowers

Flowers bring joy to your ceremony. Choose flowers that coordinate with your ceremony's theme, formality, and colors. For example, if you're planning an elegant formal wedding, you may want to include white orchids and baby's breath in your floral arrangements. However, if you're planning an informal, barefoot nature wedding, you may want to incorporate daisies and wildflowers. Your florist can make recommendations.

Here are basic floral needs for a wedding:

- Bridal bouquet
- Bridal attendants' bouquets
- Boutonnieres for all the men, including the groom, his attendants, the fathers, grandfathers, and every man or boy who will be included in

your wedding, such as a ring bearer, soloist, reader, or candle-lighter.

- Altar arrangements
- Flowergirl basket
- Corsages for mothers, grandmothers, and every female who will be included in your wedding, such as a soloist, organist, candle-lighter, or reader.
- Floral treatments for candelabra, candle sconces, pews, garlands, unity candle and tapers, and memorial wreaths/candles, if applicable.

When you meet with your florist, avoid the generic, cookie-cutter look. Take a step outside the box and think creatively. For example, instead of the traditional bridal bouquet, you may prefer to carry a decorated Bible or prayer book. Or, if you're planning a Christmas wedding, purchase giant candy canes, one for each bridesmaid to carry instead of a traditional bouquet. Bring the candy canes to your florist and ask him to decorate them with holly and trailing ribbons.

Remember that greenery can serve as attractive filler when incorporated into pew arrangements, garlands, window dressings, and any other floral arrangements.

Decorations

You may embellish your ceremony venue further with the use of ribbon, draped fabric or lace, balloons, and props.

Ribbon

Incorporate ribbon into all your floral arrangements, including those in front of the venue, on the altar, on the sconces and candelabra, at the end of each pew or row of chairs, and any floral or greenery garlands. This is another case where more is better, so don't scrimp.

Draped Fabric / Lace

Enhance the front of your venue by draping fabric or lace over the altar, wrapping around the altar railing, and incorporating into the garlands and pew arrangements, as appropriate.

Balloons

If you're planning an informal indoor or outdoor wedding, helium-filled balloons can be used to add color and joy to your venue. Use them in balloon bouquets, tied to the backs of chairs, or inserted into floral arrangements. You can also create a romantic balloon archway: simply tie clusters of helium balloons to a long fishing line, held down at each end by a fabric-covered brick or cement block. The balloon clusters will form an arch all by themselves (the law of physics, you see), creating a romantic archway for you to stand under during the ceremony.

By the way, for an outdoor ceremony, another joyful use of helium-filled balloons is to give one to each guest to hold during the ceremony. Then, after you've been pronounced husband and wife and the groom kisses his bride, the guests release their balloons into the air and applaud for the couple.

Note: Tie the balloons with biodegradable cotton string.

Props

Props are items that you purchase or rent from a wedding supply store, or borrow from a friend or relative, to help create a special ambience for your ceremony. They may or may not be theme related. Here are a few ideas:

- White garden trellis or latticework
- A decorated wedding arch
- Tissue bells
- Decorated wreaths
- Wrought iron benches
- Tiki torches
- Old-fashioned street lamps
- Carousel horses
- White pillars, urns, or candelabra
- A wishing well
- A gazebo
- Fountains
- White or gold bird cages
- White folding chairs

Lighting

Lighting is more important than you would think. If your ceremony venue comes with a lighting system, you're in luck. Some venues even provide a lighting technician who will create a charming ambience for your ceremony, including special effects. For example, as the processional begins, the overhead lights may be dimmed and a spotlight may follow the entrants down the aisle. Then, as the bride walks down the aisle, the overhead lighting is turned off completely and she is spotlighted as she enters on the arm of her father.

In addition to the lighting provided by the venue, your ceremony ambience can be enhanced with the use of candles. Candles add a special glow, so use them everywhere legally possible, especially for an evening wedding. If you're planning a candle-lighting ceremony during the prelude, enhance the ceremony by including as many candles as you can. The more candles there are to light, the more beautiful this ceremony.

Small white decorator lights, aka Christmas tree lights, also add to the charm and ambience of your ceremony venue. Borrow or purchase as many strands as you can, because more is better. Wrap them around candle sconces and candelabra and string them in and around floral or greenery garlands. These tiny lights are especially dramatic for an evening wedding.

Music

As you create your ceremony's ambience, the most powerful and touching element is the music. That's why it's important to settle for nothing less than your own unique choices—music that touches your own heart and adds poignancy to your ceremony.

As you are in the throes of planning your wedding, don't automatically accept others' recommendations for your ceremony music. Certain religious faiths don't allow a great deal of deviance from the norm, but in most situations you will have free rein to make your own selections.

Traditional musical selections used for the processional and recessional are listed in Chapters 7 and 14. Consider these selections along with any nontraditional choices available.

For the rest of your ceremony, prelude, interlude, and postlude music, as well as music for vocal performers or instrumentalist who will perform during your ceremony, consider these possibilities:

- Ave Maria (Schubert)
- Arioso (Bach)
- Larghetto (George Frideric Handel)
- Air from Water Music (George Frideric Handel)

- Clair de Lune (Claude Debussy)
- O Perfect Love (Joseph Barnby)
- I Love Thee (Grieg)
- In Thee is Joy (Johann Sebastian Bach)
- Jesu, Joy of Man's Desiring (Johann Sebastian Bach)
- The Lord's Prayer (Malotte)
- Liebestraum (Liszt)
- Love Theme from Romeo and Juliet (Tchaikovsky)
- "Follow Me" (John Denver)
- "Grow Old Along With Me" (John Lennon)
- "We've Only Just Begun" (Roger Nichols and Paul Williams)
- "Hawaiian Wedding Song" (Al Hoffman and Dick Manning)
- "Wind Beneath My Wings" (Jeff Silbar and Larry Henley)
- "Do You Remember?" (J. Ivanovici)
- "Morning Has Broken" (Eleanor Farjeon)
- "If I Didn't Have You in My World" (Vince Gill)
- "Everyday of My Life" (Aaron Neville)
- "What I Did for Love" (Marvin Hamlisch)
- "All I Ask of You" from *The Phantom of the Opera* (Webber, Hart, and Stiltoe)
- "Sunrise, Sunset" from *Fiddler on the Roof* (Sheldon Harnick and Jerry Bock)
- "Evergreen" (Barbra Streisand and Paul Williams)
- "Wedding Song" (Paul Stookey)

- ᗏ "Looking Through the Eyes of Love" (Marvin Hamlisch and Carole Bayer Sager)
- ᗏ "From This Moment" (Shania Twain and Bryan White)
- ᗏ "Endless Love" (Diana Ross and Lionel Richie)
- ᗏ "You Are the Sunshine of My Life" (Stevie Wonder)

Note: Another nice touch is to hand your guests ceremony programs as they enter the venue. See Appendix A for a sample ceremony program you may use to design your own.

Don't rush to judgment when it comes to creating the ambience for your ceremony venue. As ideas come to mind, jot them down, and you'll soon be able to envision the total picture. Keep your theme in mind as you make your decisions. I'm sure your ceremony will have a special, unique ambience that will enhance your big day.

III.

CONVENTIONAL CEREMONY ELEMENTS

When you think of a wedding, certain conventional ceremony elements come to mind:

- Ceremony seating
- Processional
- Convocation
- Invocation
- Consecration
- Expression of intent
- Vows
- Ring exchange
- Pronouncement
- Kiss
- Benediction
- Recessional

These elements may be common to religious and secular ceremonies alike. It should be noted, however, that for a marriage to be legal in the United States, these are the only three elements that are usually required:

1. The marriage vows
2. The pronouncement of marriage by a legally licensed wedding officiant
3. Two witnesses, who must sign the marriage certificate

Each state has its own specific requirements, however, so call your county marriage license bureau to find out before making your plans.

Chapter 6

CEREMONY SEATING

Certain protocol should be followed for the ceremony seating, unless the wedding is not only informal, but casual, such as a ceremony at the beach or during a Valentine's Day party.

Seating of the Guests

During the wedding ceremony, the bride's friends and family sit on the left, and the groom's on the right, unless it is a Jewish ceremony where the reverse is true.

All guests should be escorted to their pews or seats by an usher. If the usher doesn't know whether a certain guest is a friend of the bride or groom, he should ask, so that the guest may be seated on the proper side of the venue. The usher should escort the guests as follows:

- A female guest

  The usher presents his right arm to escort the guest to her seat.

- A male guest

  The usher walks on the left of the male guest as he escorts him to his seat.

∞ A female escorted by a male

The usher presents his right arm to escort the female to her seat, with the male escort following behind. Or, the usher may lead the way with the couple following behind him.

A special section of the venue may be corded off for the seating of any "Within the Ribbon" guests. These guests received small cards inside their wedding invitations inscribed with the words "within the ribbon," which they are to present to the usher when being seated. The usher recognizes the card and seats these special guests within a designated section that is usually decorated with ribbons and flowers.

Seating of the Couple's Family

The first row is reserved for the parents, with brothers, sisters, and their spouses in the second rows on each side. The third rows are reserved for grandparents and other close relatives, followed by additional relatives, and, finally, friends of the bride or groom. In a Protestant ceremony, the bride's mother is the last to be seated, to be joined by the bride's father after he has given his daughter away at the altar. She may be seated by the best man, a brother of the bride or groom, or by the head usher.

The seating of the bride's mother is a signal that the ceremony is ready to begin.

In a Jewish ceremony, the bride's and groom's parents accompany them down the aisle, then stand with the couple under the chuppah during the ceremony.

Chapter 7

PROCESSIONAL

The signal for a processional to begin is the seating of the bride's mother. The bride's mother remains seated during the processional until the moment arrives when her daughter is escorted down the aisle, at which time she stands. This is a signal for everyone to stand.

In the case of a Jewish wedding, however, the bride's mother and father escort the bride down the aisle, in which case the signal for the processional to begin is when the processional music begins.

If the ceremony has two aisles, instead of one center aisle, you may use one of the aisles and ignore the other, or you may use one for your processional and the other for your recessional.

If the groomsmen are entering during the processional, instead of entering through a side door to stand in front of the venue, the groomsmen may enter down one aisle while the bridesmaids enter down the other.

Protestant Processional

For a Protestant ceremony, the officiant, groom, best man, and groomsmen may wait at the altar as the rest of the wedding party enters in this order:

- ∞ Bridesmaids (starting with the attendant who will stand farthest from the bride)
- ∞ Maid or matron of honor
- ∞ Ring bearer
- ∞ Flower girl
- ∞ The bride, walking on the left side of her escort.

   The bride may be escorted by her father, her father and mother, her mother, her brother, or any other male relative. In the case of a bride who is close to both her father and step-father, she may be escorted down the aisle by both of them at the same time, or one may escort her halfway, and the other the rest of the way to the altar. Another popular alternative is for the groom to escort his bride down the aisle.

Note: Ushers may roll out an aisle runner after the bride's mother has been seated.

Catholic Processional

This is a suggested order for your Catholic processional (the priest, groom, and best man wait at the altar):

- ∞ The groomsmen escort the bridesmaids down the aisle, beginning with the groomsman and bridesmaid who will stand farthest from the bride and groom
- ∞ Ring bearer
- ∞ Flower girl
- ∞ Maid or matron of honor
- ∞ Bride escorted by her father (or other close male family member) on his left side

Two acceptable options:

- ∞ The priest welcomes the bride and groom and their families at the entrance to the church. He then leads the couple and their families to the altar.

- ∞ The groomsmen may enter from the side with the priest, groom, and best man, in which case the bridesmaids walk down the aisle single file.

Jewish Processional

This is a suggested order for your processional:

- ∞ The chuppah carried by four chuppah holders (if not using a freestanding chuppah)

- ∞ Rabbi

- ∞ Cantor

- ∞ Grandparents, who are ushered to their seats

- ∞ Ring bearer and flower girl

- ∞ Male and female members of the wedding party walk in pairs, men on the left and women on the right

- ∞ Maid or matron of honor

- ∞ Best man (or may walk beside the maid or matron of honor, on her left)

- ∞ Groom (flanked by his parents)

- ∞ Bride (flanked by her parents)*

  * This is practiced by Orthodox and some Conservative Jews. Reform Jews and other Conservative Jews have modified this custom so that only the bride's father walks her down the aisle.

Informal Processional Options

- The bride, groom, and their attendants enter from the side all at once and assemble themselves in front of the ceremony venue.

- The bride's and groom's family and attendants enter from the sides of the venue and then the bride and groom enter as they walk down the center aisle, or through the center of the seated guests, depending on the informality of the wedding.

- In the case of a very informal, casual ceremony, such as a barefoot wedding on a beach, the bride and groom may face the officiant, with their attendants, friends and family members clustered around them in no particular order.

Popular Musical Selections for a Processional

A list of popular processional selections follows. Don't feel compelled to choose a selection from this list, however. Unless religious restrictions apply, you may choose any musical selection you would like.

In any case, choose something uplifting and celebratory.

- Here Comes the Bride (Richard Wagner)
- Canon in D (Johann Pachelbel)
- Spring, The Four Seasons (Antonio Vivaldi)
- Trumpet Tune (Henry Purcell)
- Trumpet Voluntary (Jeremiah Clarke)
- Wedding March (Wolfgang Amadeus Mozart)
- Overture (George Frideric Handel)
- Romeo and Juliet Love Theme (Piotr Ilyitch Tchaikovsky)

- "Wedding Processional" from *The Sound of Music* by Rodgers and Hammerstein
- Triumphal March (Edvard Grieg)
- Ode to Joy (Ludwig van Beethoven)
- The Arrival of the Queen of Sheba (George Frideric Handel)
- Sonata in G Major (Giuseppi Tartini)
- Now Thank We All Our God (Johann Sebastian Bach)
- Psalm 19 (Benedetto Marcello)

Chapter 8

CONVOCATION/
INVOCATION

In a religious ceremony the convocation and invocation immediately follow the processional. Once the members of the wedding party are in place, the clergyman or officiant speaks, formally convening the marriage service, and invoking God's blessing upon it.

This chapter contains a selection of convocations and invocations, suitable for religious or secular ceremonies

Model Convocations

"We are gathered here today in the presence of these witnesses to join _____ (bride) and _____ (groom) in holy matrimony, which is commended to be honorable among all men and to be entered into reverently and discreetly."

*****

"Friends, we are here to share a very important day in the lives of _____(bride) and _____(groom)— their wedding day. We are honored to be part of this day, to witness their vows, and send them off as husband and wife, with our blessings."

*****

"Is this a happy day, or what? We can feel the love, can't we friends? What a joy to be part of your day, _____(bride) and _____(groom). We are privileged and honored to be witnesses to your vows and to shower you with our love and approval."

*****

"We are here today to witness the joining together of _____(bride) and _____(groom) in the holy estate of marriage. We are also here to celebrate with them, and to share their joy."

Model Invocations

"May the God who knows us and loves us grant blessings on _____(bride) and _____(groom) as they become husband and wife this day. And grant your blessings also to this couple's family members and friends assembled here today for this beautiful ceremony."

*****

"God, our Father in heaven, the source of all love, please be present today during this sacred ceremony. We especially ask your blessing on this couple, who stands before us, and for all of us who share their joy. May each one of us sense your love and may we be filled with your love as we witness the vows of _____(bride) and _____(groom). Amen."

*****

"Thank you for bringing____(bride) and ____(groom) together. Thank you for the love you have given them toward each other. May your love encircle them during this service, and may their marriage be richly filled with the love and joy only You can bring. Amen."

*****

"Thank you, our Father, for the gifts of love you have given ____(bride) and ____(groom). Please bless their love and their marriage. Be present here with us during this sacred ceremony. Amen."

Chapter 9

CONSECRATION AND
EXPRESSION OF INTENT

Following the convocation and invocation are the consecration and expression of intent. Each officiant, whether religious or secular, has a selection of various consecration wordings and expressions of intent. Your officiant will probably allow you to choose which wordings you want included in your ceremony. If you aren't given this option, ask.

Here are examples of a consecration and expression of intent.

Consecration

A consecration, as it pertains to a marriage ceremony, is the declaration that the ceremony be considered sanctified and dedicated to a sacred purpose. This is one example:

> "Our holy God, please sanctify the marriage vows to be spoken today by _____ (bride) and _____(groom). As their vows are spoken, may they not only dedicate themselves to each other, but to you for the sacred purpose of serving you as a married couple."

Expression of Intent

An expression of intent is exactly what it sounds like—the bride's and groom's verbal expression of intent to marry each other.

Clergyman to the bride:

"_____, is it your intent to marry _____ today? To bond to him as his wife?"

Bride:

"Yes."

Clergyman to the groom:

"_____, is it your intent to marry _____ today? To bond to her as her husband?"

Groom:

"Yes."

Chapter 10

Vows

Your wedding vows are one of the three required elements for a legal marriage.

The majority of couples opts for one of the following:

- Accepts the vow wording always used by the officiant who marries them.
- Recites the precise vow wording dictated by their religious faith.
- Chooses from several optional vow wordings suggested to them by their officiant.
- Writes personalized vows. According to a survey conducted by Bridal Guide Magazine, 21 percent of couples write their own wedding vows.

The concept of having a choice is quite new in our society. For centuries brides and grooms didn't know they were allowed to compose their own vows. However, today's couples are embracing the idea of personalizing their wedding vows, which is why I wrote the book *Diane Warner's Complete Book of Wedding Vows*, now available in its newly revised second edition. It contains traditional and nontraditional vows, vows for second marriages, vows that include children, reaffirmation vows, vows with religious variations, vows inspired by the classics, ring vows and theme wedding vows.

Included below are traditional vows, followed by a sampling of personalized vows taken from my wedding vows book.

Traditional Vows

You'll find traditional vows for a civil ceremony in Chapter 35.

Traditional religious vows for a Jewish, Catholic, or Protestant ceremony can be found in section VI.

Here are other traditional religious vow wordings:

Episcopalian

The Episcopalian Church in the United States is also known as the Protestant Episcopal Church, a body originally associated with the Church of England. This denomination tends to favor formal, traditional worship services and wedding ceremonies.

"In the Name of God, I _____, take you, _____, to be my husband/wife, to have and to hold from this day forward, for better, for worse, for richer, for poorer, in sickness and in health, to love and to cherish, until we are parted by death. This is my solemn vow."

or

"I, _____, take thee, _____, to be my wedded husband/wife, to have and to hold from this day forward, for better, for worse, for richer, for poorer, in sickness and in health, to love and to cherish, till death do us part, according to God's holy ordinance; and thereto I plight/give thee my troth."

American Lutheran

The American Lutheran Church branched out from the original Lutheran Church, a Protestant denomination founded by Martin Luther after the Reformation in the 16th century. There are many types of Lutheran churches in America, some favoring formal, traditional worship services, others a more relaxed, contemporary style, but all adhering to the Protestant religious teachings of Martin Luther. A Lutheran wedding ceremony may be formal or informal. This is one traditionally accepted wedding vow:

> "I take you, _____, to be my husband/wife from this day forward, to join with you and share all that is to come, and I promise to be faithful to you until death parts us."

Presbyterian

Although there are many types of Presbyterian churches, they all generally adhere to Calvinism, which is based on the religious doctrines of John Calvin, a 16th century French theologian and religious reformer. As is true in the Lutheran church, Presbyterian churches vary greatly in their style of worship. In the case of a formal Presbyterian wedding ceremony, however, this is an example of an acceptable vow phrasing:

> "I, _____, take you to be my wedded wife/husband, and I do promise and covenant, before God and these witnesses, to be your loving and faithful wife/husband, in plenty and in want, in joy and in sorrow, in sickness and in health, as long as we both shall live."

Methodist

The Methodist Church in America is a Protestant Christian denomination with theologies developed from the teachings of John and Charles Wesley. Their worship services, as well as their marriage ceremonies, vary greatly as to their formality. Here is one of their traditionally accepted wedding vows:

"In the Name of God, I, _____, take you, _____, to be my husband/wife, to have and to hold from this day forward, for better, for worse, for richer, for poorer, in sickness and in health, to love and to cherish, until we are parted by death. This is my solemn vow."

United Church of Christ

Although the United Church of Christ is a fairly new denomination in America, founded in 1957 by a merger of the Congregational Christian Church and the Evangelical and Reformed Church, they are direct descendants of the first permanent Protestant settlers, the Pilgrims. In their present Book of Worship, published in 1986, their denomination's preferred wedding vows are stated, reflecting the important concept of giving one's self, as different from taking another. Their vows are:

Bride:

"_____ (groom's name), I give myself to you to be your wife. I promise to love and sustain you in the covenant of marriage, from this day forward, in sickness and in health, in plenty and in want, in joy and in sorrow, as long as we both shall live."

Groom:

"_____ (bride's name), I give myself to you to be your husband. I promise to love and sustain you in the covenant of marriage, from this day forward, in sickness and in health, in plenty and in want, in joy and in sorrow, as long as we both shall live."

Unitarian / Universalist

The Unitarian Church does not offer a standard service, but leaves the composition of the service to each of its ministers. Here are two examples, however, of typical Unitarian Universalist wedding vows:

The minister asks the bride and groom:

"_____, will you take _____ to be your husband/wife; love, honor, and cherish him/her now and forevermore?"

The bride and groom answer:

"I will."

Then the minister asks the bride and groom to repeat these words:

"I,_____, take you, _____, to be my husband/wife; to have and to hold from this day forward, for better, for worse, for richer, for poorer, in sickness and in health, to love and cherish always."

The minister asks the bride and groom:

"_____, will you have _____ to be your husband/wife, to live together in creating an abiding marriage? Will you love and honor, comfort and cherish him/her in sickness and in health, in sorrow and in joy, from this day forward?"

The bride and groom answer:
"I will."

Quaker

A Quaker wedding is very simple, in keeping with the Quaker tradition. The marriage usually takes places during a regular worship meeting where all in attendance meditate silently while the bride and groom enter and join those already seated. Then, after the traditional Quaker silence, the bride and groom rise, join hands, face each other, and repeat these vows:

"In the presence of God and these our Friends I take thee to be my wife/husband, promising with Divine assistance to be unto thee a loving and faithful wife/husband so long as we both shall live."

The groom speaks his promises first, then the bride. The bride is not given away, nor does a third person pronounce them married, for the Friends believe that only God can create such a union.

Eastern Orthodox

The churches of the Eastern Rite (including Greek and Russian Orthodox) are similar in some ways to the Catholic Church. The marriage itself is a long ceremony rich with symbolism. An Orthodox wedding begins with a betrothal ritual that includes the blessing and exchange of rings. The rings are exchanged between bride and groom three times to signify the Holy Trinity. At the close of this betrothal ritual, there is the marriage rite, including the candles and the joining of hands, followed by the crowning, the cup, and finally, the triumphal procession of Isaiah. The vows themselves are spoken silently during this service, but the couple is considered married when the crowns are finally removed by the priest and he blesses them by saying:

"Be thou magnified, O bridegroom."

Muslim

Bride:

"I,_____, offer you myself in marriage in accordance with the instructions of the Holy Qur'an and the Holy Prophet, peace and blessing be upon Him. I pledge, in honesty and with sincerity, to be for you an obedient and faithful wife."

Groom:

"I pledge, in honesty and sincerity, to be for you a faithful and helpful husband."

Hinduism

Here is a modern day interpretation of the traditionally strict Indian wedding vows:

"Let us take the first steps to provide for our household a nourishing and pure diet, avoiding those foods injurious to healthy living. Let us take the second step to develop physical, mental, and spiritual powers. Let us take the third step, to increase our wealth by righteous means and proper use. Let us take the fourth step, to acquire knowledge, happiness, and harmony by mutual love and trust. Let us take the fifth step, so that we be blessed with strong, virtuous, and heroic children. Let us take the sixth step, for self-restraint and longevity. Finally, let us take the seventh step and be true companions and remain lifelong partners by this wedlock."

Carpatho Russian Orthodox

This is a sect within the Eastern Orthodox Church that allows spoken vows, as opposed to the traditional silent vows taken during most Eastern Orthodox wedding ceremonies.

"I,_____, take you, _____, as my wedded wife/husband and I promise you love, honor, and respect; to be faithful to you, and not to forsake you until death do us part. So help me God, one in the Holy Trinity, and all the Saints.'

Nondenominational Protestant

There are hundreds of Protestant churches in America that are not affiliated with any particular denomination. Here are examples of marriage vow phrasings commonly used by this type of church.

"Will you have this woman to be your wedded wife, to live together in holy matrimony? Will you love her, comfort her, honor, and keep her in sickness and in health, in sorrow and in joy, and, forsaking all others, be faithful to her as long as you both shall live?"

The groom answers:

"I do."

Then, the minister continues by asking the same of the bride.

******

The couple joins right hands and recites these traditional vows to each other, either from memory, or by prompting from the officiant:

"I take you to be my wedded wife/husband,
To have and to hold, from this day forward,

For better, for worse, for richer, for poorer,
In sickness and in health, to love and to cherish,
Till death do us part.
This is my solemn vow
According to God's holy ordinance;
And thereto I plight you my troth."

* * * * * *

"I,_____, take thee, _____, to be my wedded husband/wife, to have and to hold, from this day forward, for better, for worse, for richer, for poorer, in sickness and in health, to love and to cherish, till death us do part, according to God's holy ordinance; and thereto I pledge thee my faith."

Personalized Vows

You will find many personalized vow segments within other chapters of this book, including vows recited during the circle of acceptance, covenant of salt ceremony, ceremony of the wishing stones, encore, nature, new life, and other ceremonies.

Here is a sampling of personalized vows taken from my book, *Diane Warner's Complete Book of Wedding Vows*, 2nd edition:

Nontraditional Secular Vows

"I bring myself to you this day to share my life with you; you can trust my love, for it's real. I promise to be a faithful mate and to unfailingly share and support your hopes, dreams and goals. I vow to be there for you always; when you fall, I will catch you; when you cry, I will comfort you; when you laugh, I will share your joy. Everything I am and everything I have is yours, from this moment forth and for eternity."

******

"_____, since you came into my life, my days have been bright and glorious, but today, our wedding day, is the brightest of them all, a golden moment, made splendid by our love for each other. And yet, this beautiful moment is only a taste of what is to come as we share our lives together as husband and wife. I pledge my love to you from this day forward; I promise to be faithful and true to you, rejoicing in my good fortune to have found you as my life mate."

Vows that Include Children

Minister (addressing the groom—referring to the child):

"And do you, _____, take _____ as your own, promising to love her and care for her, providing for her needs, physical and spiritual?"

Groom:

"I do."

Minister (addressing the child):

"And do you, _____, take _____, to be your loving father from this day forward?"

The child:

"I do."

Groom (addressing the child):

"_____, I place this ring on your finger as a sign of my loving promise made this day."

Note: The bride may recite these same vows to the groom's child, also placing a ring on the child's finger.

Valentine's Day Ceremony

"It is fitting that we marry on Valentine's Day, the most romantic day of the year, when lovers celebrate their love; truly, we celebrate our love today as our hearts are joined in holy, sacred matrimony. I will hold gently the heart you have given me this day, a lasting treasure to be cherished, and I give my heart to you with joy and abandonment, as I promise to be your faithful husband/wife. Every year we will reaffirm our vows on Valentine's Day, as we celebrate our wedding day, the day we gave our hearts to each other until the end of time."

New Year's Ceremony

Bride/groom:

"As we put the past behind us and embark on a new year, so we put our individual lives behind us as we become one in holy matrimony. And just as a new year is bright and promising, so you are my new day, my hope, my joy and the sunshine of our future together. Take my hand (takes bride's/groom's hand) and walk with me into the new year and into our new life as my husband/wife. I give you my heart and everything that I am as we begin our lives together, united as one flesh."

Victorian Ceremony

The Victorian age relates to the period when Queen Victoria reigned in Britain, the mid- to late 1800s. In today's world of weddings, a Victorian wedding signifies old-fashioned romance.

Groom to his bride:

"O my Luve's like a red, red rose, that's newly sprung in June; O my Luve's like the melodie that's sweetly played in tune, as fair as thou, my bonnie lass, so deep in luve am I, and I will luve thee still, my dear, Till a'the seas gang dry. I love you _____, and I vow to be true and faithful to you 'til death do us part."

Bride to her groom:

"O my Luve's like a red, red rose, that's newly sprung in June; O my Luve's like the melodie that's sweetly played in tune, as fair as thou, my handsome lad, so deep in luve am I, and I will luve thee still, my dear, Till a'the seas gang dry. I love you _____, and I vow to be true and faithful to you 'til death do us part."

[Words adapted from a poem by Robert Burns.]

Renaissance Ceremony

The Renaissance age, A.D. 1450 to A.D. 1600, is the period when Christopher Columbus sailed to the New World, and the infamous Henry VIII reigned in England. Renaissance festivals are extremely popular today, depicting this age of chivalry, when a Lady presented her Knight with her scarf or handkerchief to wear on his sleeve when he went into a battle or a joust.

Here is an example of Renaissance ceremony wedding vows:

Lord _____ (groom):

"I taketh thy hand in mine, my lady, my truest love, and looketh upon thy gracious countenance, as I pledgeth mine oath and troth to thee in vow of matrimony. I forsake mine ancient ways, and all others from mine past, to cleave unto thee, for all eternities to come, as thy devoted husband. Before these goode witnesses, I giveth myself to thee this day, to be thy protectorate and thy sustainer throughout all our lives. From this day forth, may we be not two, but one. I loveth thee, my Lady _____ (bride)."

Lady _____(bride):

"I accept thy pledge, my Lord, my love, and I also pledgeth mine oath and troth to thee in vow of matrimony. I shall loveth thee and careth for thee all the days of our lives. Before these goode witnesses, I giveth myself to thee this day, to joineth with thee as we be not two, but one, for all eternity. I loveth thee, mine Lord _____ (groom)."

Note: The marriage vows may be read from a parchment scroll on which the vows have been written with a black calligraphy pen. After the ceremony, this scroll may be framed as a memento of the wedding.

Vows Inspired by the Classics

Come live with me, and be my love,
And we will some new pleasures prove
Of golden sands, and crystal brooks,
With silken lines, and silver hooks
—John Donne

******

How do I love thee? Let me count the ways.
I love thee to the depth and breadth and height

My soul can reach, when feeling out of sight
For the ends of Being and ideal Grace.
I love thee to the level of everyday's
Most quiet need, by sun and candle light.
I love thee freely, as men strive for Right;
I love thee purely, as they turn from Praise.
I love thee with the passion put to use
In my old griefs, and with my childhood's faith.
I love thee with a love I seemed to lose
With my lost saints,—I love thee with the breath,
Smiles, tears, of all my life!—and, if God choose,
I shall but love thee better after death.

—*Inspired by the words of Elizabeth Barrett Browning, from* "Sonnets from the Portuguese"

Old Indian Wedding Verses

"Now we feel no rain, for each of us will be shelter to the other. Now we will feel no cold, for each of us will be warmth to the other. Now there is no loneliness for us. Now we are two bodies, but only one life. We go now to our dwelling place, to enter into the days of our togetherness. May our days be good and long upon this earth."

—Based on an Apache Indian prayer

"You are my husband/wife
My feet shall run because of you.
My feet, dance because of you.
My eyes, see because of you.
My mind, think because of you.
And I shall love because of you."

—Old Eskimo Indian wedding vow

I hope you found inspiration from the vow wordings included in this chapter. Perhaps you love one of the segments so much, you'd like to adopt it as is, or maybe you would like to adopt a phrase here and there, combine them, and call them your own.

You may decide to take a look at my wedding vows book, where you'll find hundreds of choices. Whatever you decide, I hope the vows you include in your ceremony are poignant and meaningful.

Chapter 11

RING EXCHANGE

The wedding ring is seen as a seal upon the wedding vow, a symbol of the couple's lifetime commitment to one another. It is also seen by some to be a religious symbol of the holiness and sacredness of marriage, as ordained by God. This chapter contains a variety of ring vows, some traditional, and many nontraditional, because it has become popular for the bride and groom to write their own personalized ring vows, as well as the wedding vows themselves.

Jewish Ring Vows

Rabbi (addressing the bridegroom):

"Then, _____, put this ring upon the finger of your bride and say to her: 'Be thou consecrated to me, as my wife, by this ring, according to the Law of Moses and of Israel.'"

The Rabbi then asks the bride to repeat the following:

"May this ring I receive from thee be a token of my having become thy wife according to the Law of Moses and of Israel."

If two rings are used, the bride may say:

"This ring is a symbol that thou art my husband in accordance with the Law of Moses and Israel."

Catholic Ring Vows

The priest blesses the rings:

"Blessing of the Wedding Rings

Our help is in the name of the Lord.

Who made heaven and earth.

O Lord, hear my prayer.

And let my cry come unto Thee.

The Lord be with you.

And with your spirit."

Priest (to the couple):

"Now that you have sealed a truly Christian marriage, give these wedding rings to each other, saying after me:"

Groom (addressing his bride):

"In the name of the Father, and of the Son, and of the Holy Spirit. Take and wear this ring as a pledge of my fidelity."

Bride (addressing her bridegroom):

"In the name of the Father, and of the Son, and of the Holy Spirit. Take and wear this ring as a pledge of my fidelity."

American Lutheran Ring Vows

"I give you this ring as a sign of my love and faithfulness."

Episcopalian Ring Vows

Groom/bride:

"_____, I give you this ring as a symbol of my vow, and with all that I am, and all that I have, I honor you, in the Name of the Father, and of the Son, and of the Holy Spirit (or 'in the Name of God')."

Presbyterian Ring Vows

Groom/bride:

"This ring I give you, in token and pledge, of our constant faith, and abiding love."

or

"With this ring I thee wed, in the name of the Father, and of the Son, and of the Holy Spirit. Amen."

Methodist Ring Vows

Groom/bride:

"_____, I give you this ring as a sign of my vow, and with all that I am, and all that I have, I honor you."

United Church of Christ Ring Vows

"This ring I give you in token of my faithfulness and love, and as a pledge to honor you with my whole being and to share with you my worldly goods."

or

"I give you this ring in token of the covenant made today between us; in the name of the Father, and of the Son, and of the Holy Spirit."

United Church of Canada Ring Vows

"_____, I give you this ring that you may wear it as a symbol of our marriage."

Unitarian / Universalist Ring Vows

The minister repeats these words as the rings are exchanged between the bride and groom:

"As a token of mutual fidelity and affection the ring(s) are now given and received."

The bride and groom, if they wish, may repeat their own ring vows:

"With this ring, I wed you and pledge you my love now and forever."

or

"Be consecrated to me, with this ring, as my wife/ husband in accordance with the faith of our loved ones."

Catholic / Non-Catholic Ring Vows

"_____, take this ring as a sign of my love and fidelity. In the name of the Father, and of the Son, and of the Holy Spirit."

Jewish / Christian Ring Vows

"Be thou consecrated unto me with this ring as my wife/husband, according to the faith of God and humanity."

Nondenominational Ring Vows

Groom:

"I offer you this ring as a sign of my love and fidelity. It will always be a symbol of the vows which have made us husband and wife here this morning."

Bride:

"I accept this ring as a symbol of our love and wear it proudly as your wife."

*****

"Dear _____, with this ring I thee wed, and by it be thou consecrated unto me, as my wedded wife/husband according to the laws of God and of man."

*****

"With this ring I wed you and pledge my faithful love. I take you as my husband/wife and pledge to share my life openly with you, to speak the truth to you in love. I promise to honor and tenderly care for you, to cherish and encourage your fulfillment as an individual through all the changes of our lives."

*****

Minister:

"Now, may I have a token of your sincerity that you will keep these vows?"

(The best man gives the bride's ring to the minister who then holds it up and says:)

"From the beginning of time, the ring has symbolized many kinds of human relationships. Kings wore them to express their imperial authority; friends exchanged them as expressions of their good will; high school and college graduates wore them as expressions of their school loyalties. This simple band of gold, however, has come to its highest significance as a symbol of a marriage relationship. Wearing it bears witness to your marital fidelity."

(The minister hands the bride's ring to the groom and instructs him to place it on her finger.)

Minister (to the groom):

"Do you, _____, give this ring to _____ as a token of your love for her?"

Groom:

"I do."

Minister (to the bride):

"Will you, _____, take this ring from _____ as a token of his love for you and will you wear it as an expression of your love for him?"

Bride:

"I will."

(The minister takes the groom's ring from the maid or matron of honor or from the ring bearer and gives it to the bride, instructing her to place it on the groom's finger.)

Minister (to the bride):

"Do you, _____, give this ring to _____ as an expression of your love for him?"

Bride:

"I do."

Minister (to the groom):

"Will you, _____, take this ring from _____ as a token of her love for you and will you wear it as an expression of your love for her?"

Groom:

"I will."

*****

"I bring this ring as a symbol of my love and fidelity as your husband/wife, and as I slide it onto your finger, I commit my very heart and soul to you, my dear husband/wife, and I ask you to wear it as a reminder of the vows we have taken today."

*****

"With this ring I thee wed, in the Name of God. Amen."

*****

"With this ring I wed thee and I accept thee as my husband/wife; I take thee as my partner in life and I hereby endow thee with all my worldly goods."

*****

"May this ring be a permanent reminder of our holy promises and steadfast love, through Jesus Christ our Lord. Amen."

*****

"_____, this ring is the sign of my love and faithfulness, and I give it to you in the name of the Father, the Son and the Holy Spirit. Amen."

*****

"Thou art my beloved and I give thee this ring as a visible reminder to you and all who see it that my love for you is constant and eternal."

*****

"You are my life, my love, my best friend and with this ring I wed thee; may it be a reminder of my love and the sacred commitment I have made here today."

*****

"When we were in high school, I gave you my class ring and you wore it on a chain around your neck to show the world that we were going steady. But today I give you something much more precious: a wedding ring; may it be a sign to all who see it that we're going steady for the rest of our lives and that you belong to me alone."

*****

"As this ring encircles your finger from this day forward, year in and year out, so will my love forever encircle you. Wear this ring as a symbol of this love."

*****

"With this ring I seal the commitment I have made to you today; may you wear it proudly as my wife/husband."

*****

"_____, take this ring as a seal upon the marriage vows I have spoken and, as you wear it, may it be a reminder of how much I love you, not only on this precious day, but every single day of your life."

*****

"This ring is the visible evidence of our invisible love; it symbolizes the joining of our spirits in sacred holy matrimony."

*****

"As I place this ring on your finger, its perfect symmetry is a symbol of our perfect love. It has no beginning and no ending, a symbol of the eternal commitment we have made to each other today."

*****

"This ring is round and hath no end,
So is my love unto my friend."
—16th-century verse

*****

"Our love is even more precious than this diamond (or whatever stone the bride wears in her engagement ring), and more enduring than this band of gold, but I place this band on your finger as a symbol of our love and the vows we have spoken here today."

*****

"Just as this ring is made from precious metal, sturdy and strong, so will our marriage be: a precious commitment to each other that remains sturdy and strong until death do us part."

*****

"This ring is enduring evidence of my enduring love and its purity is a symbol of the sacredness of our vows."

*****

"Today we are on a mountaintop; everything is good and happy and right. But someday there will be valleys as well, and as we walk through those valleys together, may this ring be a reminder of this mountaintop experience, and the vows we have made this day."

*****

"Just as our love is shining and pure, so is this golden wedding ring, an emblem of the lifelong commitment I have made to you this day."

*****

"With this ring I wed you—not only for today, our wedding day, so all may see its golden glow; but for all our tomorrows, until death do us part. Wear it as a sign of my love for you and a notice to the world that you have chosen me to be your husband/wife."

*****

"_____, with this ring I wed you; with my body I worship you, and with all my worldly goods I endow you."

*****

"As a sign of my commitment and the desire of my heart, I give you this ring. May it always be a reminder that I have chosen you above all other women/men and that, from this day forward, you are my wife/husband."

*****

Minister:

"I hold in my hand two beautiful rings, symbolic of a binding contract, to be given and received as bonds of neverending love and devoted friendship, circles of life and circles of love."

(The minister hands one of the rings to the groom who places it on his bride's finger.)

Groom:

"With this ring I wed thee and offer it as a symbol of our everlasting love."

(The minister hands the other ring to the bride who places it on her groom's finger.)

Bride:

"With this ring I wed thee and offer it as a symbol of our everlasting love."

*****

"_____, I give you this ring as a symbol, not only of my love for you and my promise to be your faithful husband/wife, but as a reminder that God is also part of our marriage, to be honored and praised every day of our lives."

*****

"_____, whenever the world sees this ring on your finger, it will be a symbol of my love for you and that, although I may not be present with you at that moment, I am always faithful to you, honoring you and cherishing you as my husband/wife."

*****

"This wedding band is a perfect circle of precious metal that symbolizes a man's kingdom and his earthly possessions, and as I place this ring on your finger, I entrust you with my kingdom and possessions. When you look at this ring in the years to come, may it remind you of my vows to you this day and may you always feel encircled by my love, just as this band encircles your finger."

*****

"_____, I give you this ring as a symbol of my love for you. Let it remind you always, as it circles your finger, of my eternal love, surrounding you and enfolding you day and night."

*****

"You are my beloved bride/bridegroom and I marry you today with this ring as I give you my heart, my body and the very breath of my soul."

*****

"Just as this gold band wraps endlessly around your finger, so shall my love always wrap around the very breath of your soul; may it be a reminder of the sacred vows I have spoken this day."

*****

Minister (to the bride and groom):

"I will ask you now to seal the vows which you have just made by the giving and receiving of rings. Let us remember that the circle is the emblem of eternity and it is our prayer that your love and happiness will be as unending as the rings which you exchange."

Minister (to the groom):

"_____, do you have a token of your love?"

Groom:

"Yes, a ring."

(The best man gives the ring to the minister; the minister gives it to the groom; the groom places it on his bride's finger and then repeats after the minister:)

"This ring I give thee, in token and pledge, of our constant faith, and abiding love."

Minister (to the bride):

"_____, do you have a token of your love?"

Bride:

"Yes, a ring."

(The maid or matron of honor gives the ring to the minister; the minister gives it to the bride; the bride then places it on the finger of the groom and repeats after the minister:)

"This ring I give thee, in token and pledge, of our constant faith, and abiding love."

*****

"Go little ring to that same sweet
That hath my heart in her domain..."
—Geoffrey Chaucer

Ring Vows With the Covenant of Salt

Minister:

"For centuries, rings have symbolized the sealing of covenants and commitments."

(The best man gives the bride's ring to the minister who then holds it up and says:)

"This ring is a circle; it symbolizes the continuity of the marriage bond—a marriage for as long as you both shall live."

(The minister hands the bride's ring to the groom and instructs him to place it on her finger.)

Minister (to the groom):

"Do you, _____, give this ring to _____ as a token of your love for her?"

Groom:

"I do."

Minister:

"Then, as a ceaseless reminder of this hour and of the vows you have taken, _____, place this ring on the hand of your bride and repeat after me:"

Groom (repeating after the minister):

"With this ring I thee wed, with loyal love I thee endow, and all my worldly goods with thee I share, in the name of the Father and the Son and the Holy Spirit. Amen."

(The minister takes the groom's ring from the maid or matron of honor or from the ring bearer and holds it up.)

Minister:

"This ring has not always been the beautiful gold that we see here today. It came from the ground as rough ore—that ore had to be tried by a refiner fire—to drive away the impurities; now only the precious gold remains. May this ring be a symbol of difficult times. Problems will come in your marriage, but they can be like the refiner fire that drives away the impurities—leaving only the precious gold of your love, a love that shall grow more precious and beautiful as years pass by."

(The minister hands the ring to the bride.)

Minister (to the bride):

"Do you, _____, give this ring to _____ as an expression of your love for him?"

Bride:

"I do."

Minister (to the groom):

"Will you, _____, take this ring from _____ as a token of her love for you and will you wear it as an expression of your love for her?"

Groom:

"I will."

Minister (to the bride):

"Then, as a ceaseless reminder of this hour and of the vows you have taken, _____, place this ring on the hand of your groom and repeat after me."

Bride (repeating after the minister):

"With this ring I thee wed; intreat me not to leave thee or to return from following after thee, for whither thou goest I will go and where thou lodgest I will lodge: thy people shall be my people and thy God my God."

Minister (to the bride and groom):

"_____ and _____, you have just sealed your covenant by the giving and receiving of rings, and this covenant is a relationship agreement between two parties who agree that they will commit themselves to one another for the keeping of their partnership throughout their lives. The most beautiful example of this partnership is the marriage relationship. You have committed here today to share the rest of your lives with each other and that nothing, save death, will ever cause you to part. You entered this relationship as two distinct individuals, but from this day forth your lives will be so totally melded together that you will never be able to separate.

"This covenant relationship is symbolized through the pouring of these two individual bags of salt—one representing you, _____, and all that you were, all that you are and all that you will ever be, and the other representing you, _____, and all that you were and all that you are, and all that you will ever be. As these two bags of salt are poured into the third bag, the individual bags of salt will no longer exist, but will be joined together as one. Just as these grains of salt can never be separated and poured again into the individual bags, so will your marriage be. Far more important than your individuality is now the reality that you are no longer two, but one, never to be separated one from the other."

(The bride and groom each empties his/her individual bag of salt into a third bag.)

"_____ and_____, we have heard your vows and you've symbolized your union by pledging your lives to each other, exchanging rings and through the Covenant of Salt. So, by the authority of God's word and the state of _____, as a minister of the Gospel, I now pronounce you husband and wife."

Renaissance Ceremony Ring Vows

Lord _____(groom):

"My dearest Lady wife, this ring doth represent my neverending love for thee for all eternities to come. May it beareth witness to all who behold this golden circlet on thy finger that we two be bonded in sacred matrimony."

Lady_____(bride):

"I thank thee for thy most valued golden circlet representing thy love. I now placeth on thine finger a symbol of mine love and vow, as witness to all that I and thee be bonded in sacred matrimony."

Note: The marriage and ring vows may be read from a parchment scroll on which the vows have been written with a black calligraphy pen. After the ceremony, this scroll may be framed as a memento of the wedding.

Reaffirmation Ceremony Ring Vows

"We have lived and loved as we promised long ago in the presence of God, and our past and our future are a circle unbroken...like this ring, with which I renew my pledge to you of never-ending devotion."

Chapter 12

PRONOUNCEMENT AND KISS

A wedding officiant, whether religious or secular, usually uses certain wording for the pronouncement of marriage, although you may be given a choice of wordings. Here is an example of a pronouncement:

Officiant:

"May you keep this covenant you have made. May you bless each other in your marriage, comforting each other when one needs comfort, sharing each other's joys when one needs someone to share it, and helping each other in all your endeavors throughout your married lives together. And now, by the power vested in me by the laws of the state of _____, I pronounce you husband and wife."

At the end of the pronouncement, the officiant usually says to the groom:

"You may kiss your bride."

Chapter 13

BENEDICTION

The benediction is pronounced after the pronouncement of marriage and the kiss. Here are three examples of benedictions:

Clergyman:

"Whom God hath joined together, let no one put asunder. May the Lord bless you and keep you. May the Lord make His face shine upon you and be gracious unto you. May the Lord lift up His countenance unto you, and give you peace.

*****

Clergyman:

"Dear God, bless _____ and _____ as they leave this place, and bless the family and friends who have come here today to share in this great day. May the Lord go with you all."

*****

Clergyman:

"Bless this marriage we pray. May it be filled with happiness and love. Please walk beside _____(bride) and _____(groom) for all of their days together, and may their home be a place of peace and harmony. Amen."

Following the benediction, the officiant may announce you to the guests with these words:

"May I present to you Mr. and Mrs. _____."

Chapter 14

RECESSIONAL

Protestant, Catholic, and Jewish recessionals usually follow traditional orders, which follow. For an informal wedding, you may recess in any order you like, using the Protestant, Catholic, and Jewish recessionals as examples. A casual wedding ceremony doesn't require a recessional at all—family and friends simply cluster around the bride and groom to offer their congratulations.

Protestant Recessional

This is a suggested order for a Protestant recessional:

- ∞ Bride and groom
- ∞ Flower girl and ring bearer
  The flower girl may exit first, followed behind by the ring bearer, or the flower girl and ring bearer may exit walking side by side.
- ∞ Maid/matron of honor and best man
  They may exit walking side by side.

∞ Bridesmaids and groomsmen
The bridesmaids may exit side by side first, followed by the groomsmen in like manner, or the groomsmen may escort the bridesmaids, exiting in pairs.

∞ Junior attendants
They may exit in single file or walking side by side.

Catholic Recessional

A Catholic recessional is in this order:

∞ Bride and groom (bride at groom's left)

∞ Flower girl and ring bearer (optional)

∞ Honor attendants (maid/matron of honor and best man)

∞ Bridesmaids and groomsmen, in pairs

Jewish Recessional

This is a suggested order for a Jewish recessional:

∞ Bride and groom

∞ Bride's parents

∞ Groom's parents

∞ Maid or matron of honor on the arm of the best man

∞ Male and female members of the wedding party, walking in pairs

∞ Ring bearer and flower girl, walking side by side

∞ Cantor

∞ Rabbi

- The chuppah carried by four chuppah holders (if not using a freestanding chuppah)

Popular Musical Selections for a Recessional

- Canon in D (Johann Pachelbel)
- Trumpet Voluntary (Jeremiah Clarke)
- Overture from Royal Fireworks Music (George Frideric Handel)
- "Wedding Processional" from *The Sound of Music* (Rodgers and Hammerstein)
- Hallelujah Chorus (George Frideric Handel)
- Trumpet Tune and Bell Symphony (Henry Purcell)
- Badinerie from Orchestral Suite No. 2 (Johann Sebastian Bach)
- Coronation March from Crown Imperial (Sir William Walton)
- Coronation March for Czar Alexander III (Tchaikovsky)
- Promedate from *Pictures at an Exhibition* (Mussorgsky)
- Toccato from *L'Orfeo* (Monteverdi)
- Exultate, Jubilate (Wolfgang Amadeus Mozart)
- Triumphal March (Grieg)
- Ode to Joy (Ludwig van Beethoven)
- The Arrival of the Queen of Sheba (George Frideric Handel)

Note: As with your selection of processional music, feel free to select music of your own choice unless, of course, there are religious restrictions.

IV.

OPTIONAL CEREMONY ELEMENTS

Conventional ceremony elements were described in the preceding section. In addition to the conventional elements, you may decide to choose one or more of these options:

- Candle-lighting prelude
- Readings
- Officiant's address or homily
- Lighting of the unity candle

Give each of these elements some thought—don't include anything just because it's the thing to do. After reading the chapters included in this section, you'll be able to decide which, if any, will add meaning to your ceremony.

Chapter 15

CANDLE-LIGHTING PRELUDE

A candle-lighting prelude is a nice way to settle the guests down and set the stage for your ceremony. You can make it into quite a production by providing an abundance of candles to be lighted. Add candles to sconces, candelabra, along the altar railing, within floral arrangements, or anywhere else you can.

Candle-lighters may be boys or girls, teenagers, men or women. Keep in mind that if you have more people than you can use as attendants, this is a nice way to include these friends or relatives in your wedding. Whomever you choose, they should be dressed in attire that is complementary to that worn by the bridesmaids and groomsmen. By complementary I mean, for example, that the candle-lighters' gowns shouldn't match the bridesmaids' exactly, but may be similar in style and color.

You may choose a musical selection from Chapter 5 for this prelude, or you may choose one of your favorite contemporary pieces, unless religious restrictions forbid it. Whatever selection you choose, it should begin about five minutes before the candle-lighters enter the venue. This should quiet the guests who may have been chatting while waiting for the ceremony to begin.

The candle-lighters enter from the rear, walking slowly down each side of the venue. They light any candles mounted on sconces long the sides of the venue, then meet in front to light the rest of the candles mounted on candelabra or along the altar railings. After all the candles have been lighted, the candle-lighters walk slowly to the far left and right of the venue where they may stand throughout the ceremony, or they may exit the venue.

Unless you are planning an informal wedding, I highly recommend including a candle-lighting prelude to your wedding ceremony. It's a lovely way to set the tone for your wedding.

Be sure to add the names of the candle-lighters to your ceremony program, if you have one.

Note: You must follow any open flame laws or regulations that may be applicable for your ceremony venue.

Chapter 16

READINGS

A reading may be a portion of classical literature, verses of scripture, song lyrics, poetry, a personal anecdote, or a love letter. It may be read by anyone, including the bride and groom or their parents. A reading is an optional element, so it's entirely up to you whether a reading should be included in your ceremony.

If you decide to include a reading, it may be placed anywhere within the ceremony; however, it is usually placed between the invocation and the address. You also have the option of sprinkling several readings throughout your ceremony, each delivered by a different individual.

I wish I could be there with you in person to help you choose something touching, poignant, and appropriate for your ceremony. Unfortunately, I can't be there in person, but I can offer a few readings for you to consider. I hope you find something that tugs at your heart.

Favorite Ceremony Readings

Go seek her out all courteously
And say I come,
Wind of spices whose song is ever

Epithalamium.
O hurry over the dark lands
And run upon the sea
For seas and land shall not divide us
My love and me.
Now, wind, of your good courtesy
I pray you go,
And come into her little garden
And sing at her window;
Singing: The bridal wind is blowing
For Love is at his noon;
And soon will your true love be with you,
Soon, O soon.
—James Joyce from his poem "XIII, Chamber Music"

*****

How do I love thee? Let me count the ways.
I love thee to the depth and breadth and height
My soul can reach, when feeling out of sight
For the ends of Being and ideal Grace.
I love thee to the level of everyday's
Most quiet need, by sun and candlelight.
I love thee freely, as men strive for Right;
I love thee purely, as they turn from Praise.
I love thee with the passion put to use
In my old griefs, and with my childhood's faith.
I love thee with a love I seemed to lose
With my lost saints,—I love thee with the breath,
Smiles, tears, of all my life!—and, if God choose,
I shall but love thee better after death.
—Inspired by the words of Elizabeth Barrett Browning,
    from "Sonnets from the Portuguese"

*****

Now we feel no rain, for each of us will be shelter to the other. Now we will feel no cold, for each of us will be warmth to the other. Now there is no loneliness for us. Now we are two bodies, but only one life. We go now to our dwelling place, to enter into the days of our togetherness. May our days be good and long upon this earth.

—Based on an Apache Indian prayer

* * * * *

Let me not to the marriage of true minds
Admit impediments. Love is not love
Which alters when it alteration finds,
Or bends with the remover to remove:
O, no! It is an everfix'd mark,
That looks on tempests and is never shaken;
It is the star to every wandering bark,
Whose worth's unknown, although his height be taken.
Love's not Time's fool, though rosy lips and cheeks
Within his bending sickle's compass come;
Love alters not with his brief hours and weeks,
But bears it out even to the edge of doom.
If this be error and upon me prov'd,
I never writ, nor no man ever lov'd.

—Shakespearean sonnet 116

* * * * *

Two are better than one; because they have a good reward for their labour. For if they fall, the one will lift up his fellow; but woe to him that is alone when he falleth; for he hath not another to help him up. Again, if two lie together, then they have heat; but how can one be warm alone? And if one prevail against him, two shall withstand him; and a threefold cord is not quickly broken.

—Ecclesiastes 4:912

* * * * *

The Fountains mingle with the River
And the Rivers with the Oceans,
The winds of Heaven mix forever
With a sweet emotion;
Nothing in the world is single;
All things by a law divine
In one spirit meet and mingle.
"Why not I with thine?"

See the mountains kiss high Heaven
And the waves clasp one another;
No sisterflower would be forgiven
If it disdained its brother,
And the sunlight clasps the earth
And the moonbeams kiss the sea:
What is all this sweet work worth
If thou kiss not me?
—Percy Bysshe Shelley

*****

Love one another, but make not a bond of love:

Let it rather be a moving sea between the shores of your souls.

Fill each other's cup but drink not from one cup.

Give one another of your bread but eat not from the same loaf.

Sing and dance together and be joyous, but let each one of you be alone,

Even as the strings of a lute are alone though they quiver with the same music.

Give your hearts, but not into each other's keeping.

For only the hand of Life can contain your hearts.

And stand together yet not too near together:

For the pillars of the temple stand apart,

And the oak tree and the cypress grow not in each other's shadow.

—Kahlil Gibran

*****

And the Lord God caused a deep sleep to fall upon Adam, and he slept: and he took one of his ribs, and closed up the flesh instead thereof; and the rib, which the Lord God had taken from man, made he a woman, and brought her unto the man. And Adam said, This is now bone of my bones, and flesh of my flesh: she shall be called Woman, because she was taken out of Man. Therefore shall a man leave his father and his mother and shall cleave unto his wife: and they shall be one flesh.

—Genesis 2:21–24

*****

Come live with me and be my love,

And we will all the pleasures prove

That valleys, groves, hills, and fields,

Woods, or steepy mountain yields.

And we will sit upon the rocks

Seeing the shepherds feed their flocks,

By shallow rivers, to whose falls

Melodious birds sing madrigals.

And I will make thee beds of roses

And a thousand fragrant posies,

A cap of flowers and a kirtle

Embroider'd all with leaves of myrtle.
A gown made of the finest wool,
Which from our pretty lambs we pull;
Fair lined slippers for the cold,
With buckles of the purest gold.

A belt of straw and ivy buds,
With coral clasps and amber studs:
And if these pleasures may thee move,
Come live with me and be my love.

The shepherd swains shall dance and sing
For thy delight each May morning:
If these delights thy mind may move,
Then live with me and be my love.
—Christopher Marlowe

*****

Ruth said:
"Entreat me not to leave thee,
Or to return from following after thee:
For wither thou goest, I will go,
And where thou lodgest, I will lodge.
Thy people shall be my people,
And thy God my God.
Where thou diest, will I die,
And there will I be buried.
The Lord do so to me, and more also,
If ought but death part thee and me."
—Ruth 1:16–17

*****

May the road rise up to meet you.
May the wind be always at your back.
May the sun shine warm upon your face,
The rains fall soft on your fields.
And until we meet again, may the Lord
Hold you in the hollow of his hand.

Don't walk in front of me,
I may not follow.
Don't walk behind me,
I may not lead.
Walk beside me,
And just be my friend.

May we travel together through time.
We alone count as none, but together we're one,
For our partnership puts love to rhyme.
—Traditional Irish Wedding Blessing

Helpful Advice

- ∞ If you're planning a religious ceremony, talk to your officiant before selecting a reading. You may be given a list of acceptable readings to consider. For example, during a Jewish ceremony, the Seven Blessings may be read by seven family members.

- ∞ If you're planning a period wedding, consider poems and literature written during that time period in history.

- ∞ Give consideration to writing your own original poem or essay, straight from your heart. Or you can combine phrases from several wedding readings, song lyrics, love letters, or writings by your favorite authors or poets.

∞ You may choose a friend or relative to read your selection, or the reading may have such tender meaning that you decide to read it yourself. In any case, it's imperative for the reader to practice ahead of time, first, in front of a mirror, and then before friends or family members. The reading should be delivered in a firm voice, with confidence and ease.

∞ Your selections may be printed within your ceremony programs, or they may be copied onto parchment paper, which can be rolled into scrolls, tied with ribbons, and given to your guests as mementos of your wedding.

I know that you're knee deep in details right now, and you may be tempted to choose the first reading that comes along, or to omit a reading altogether, just so you can check it off your to-do list. Don't give in to this temptation, however. Take your time. Think about it. Don't make a hasty decision. Remember, when your big day finally arrives, and you're surrounded by your family and friends, you'll want every ceremony element to be poignant and meaningful. If you choose your readings with care, your wedding day memories will be sweet for all the years to come.

Chapter 17

OFFICIANT'S ADDRESS
OR HOMILY

If you choose to include an address or homily as part of your ceremony, here are two examples of an officiant's address, one secular and one religious.

Secular Address

Officiant (addressing the bride and groom):

"We are here to share your wedding day, the most important day of your lives, as we witness your vows and share in your joy. When you leave here today, you will be husband and wife, launching into your future together as one.

"From now on, your thoughts and concerns will be shared. Your lives will be intertwined as one. No longer will you think only about your personal needs, what errands you must run, or what you plan to do after you get off work. You'll think instead about each other, concerned about each other's needs, plans, and goals. You will identify with each other, feel part of each other, to the point where you'll know the other's answer before you even ask.

"Your troubles will now become our troubles. Your health problem will now become our health problem. Your projects will become our projects, and your individual joys will be shared as one.

"Encourage each other, cooperate with each other, praise each other and respect each other. Marriage is a sharing of two lives, the giving and receiving of love. And if you are so blessed as to have children born from this marriage, may you raise them and nurture them with these same qualities of unselfish love."

Religious Address

Clergyman (addressing the bride and groom):

"We are here today because of a miracle, the miracle of your love,_____(bride) and _____(groom). Marriage was established by God, our Father, as we read in chapter 2 of the book of Genesis:

'And the Lord God caused a deep sleep to fall upon Adam, and he slept: and he took one of his ribs, and closed up the flesh instead thereof; and the rib, which the Lord God had taken from man, made he a woman, and brought her unto the man. And Adam said, This is now bone of my bones, and flesh of my flesh: she shall be called Woman, because she was taken out of Man. Therefore shall a man leave his father and his mother and shall cleave unto his wife: and they shall be one flesh.'

"God didn't form Eve from Adam's foot, that he may stomp on her, or from his head, that he may rule over her, but from his side, that she may be his helpmate and companion.

"I know that your deep abiding love for each other comes from God above, for God is love, and your love is to be nurtured, cherished, and expanded every day, as you draw closer to each other and closer to God. For marriage is not merely the act of living together and pleasing each other, but of living for God and pleasing Him.

"May you be each other's comfort and strength, as God guards and protects you all the days of your life. Listen to each other, encourage each other, respect each other and stand by each other's side as you walk together as husband and wife. Put God first in your marriage, always seeking His will, as you abide in love, just as the love chapter describes:

'Love is patient, love is kind. It does not envy, it does not boast, it is not proud. It is not rude, it is not selfseeking, it is not easily angered, it keeps no record of wrongs. Love does not delight in evil, but rejoices with the truth. It always protects, always hopes, always perseveres. Where there are prophecies, they will cease; where there are tongues, they will be stilled; where there is knowledge, it will pass away, but love never fails. And now these three remain: Faith, Hope and Love, but the greatest of these is Love.'

My prayer for you, and I'm sure the prayers of your friends and family assembled here today, is that your marriage will always be beautiful. Always new. May it be protected by God's love, and may no one ever disturb your holy union. God bless you both."

Chapter 18

LIGHTING OF THE UNITY CANDLE

The lighting of the unity candle has become a popular addition to the wedding ceremony because of its deep meaning. It has several variations, including the traditional lighting by the bride and groom; participation by the couple's parents; and participation by the couple's children.

Lighting by the Bride and Groom

After the bride and groom have recited their wedding vows, they walk together to the unity candle, which is a large candle that sits unlighted between two smaller lighted candles. The two smaller candles represent their individual lives and families. The bride and groom each lift a smaller candle and, together, light the larger unity candle, symbolizing their marriage to each other and that two families have become one.

Note: The bride and groom may extinguish their individual candles, signifying that they are no longer individuals, but are united as one; or, after lighting the unity candle, they may leave their individual candles lighted, signifying that although they are united in marriage, they have not lost their individuality.

The unity candle may be personalized with the couple's names and their wedding date, allowing it to be kept as a treasured keepsake.

This ceremony may be conducted in silence or with soft music as accompaniment. See Chapter 5 for suitable musical selections.

Lighting by the Bride and Groom and Their Parents

A variation of this ceremony is for the parents of the bride and groom to participate. The bride's parents help hold their daughter's candle as the flame is used to light the unity candle. The groom's parents do the same as they help hold their son's candle.

Another variation is for the mothers of the bride and groom to use long matches to light the tapers, symbolic of having given life to their respective children. The bride and groom proceed to use their taper to light the unity candle.

Lighting by the Bride and Groom and Their Children

A family unity candle ceremony is similar to those described previously, except that there are additional candles—one for each child. The bride, groom, and children light the central candle at the same time, symbolizing they have formed a new family unit, unified as one.

A variation of this procedure is for the bride and her children to hold one candle, and the groom and his children to hold the other candle. These two candles are used to light the unity candle at the same time.

Another poignant variation is for the bride and groom to light the central candle from their respective candles, then light their children's candles from the wick of the central candle.

Note: The lighting of this candle may be silent, or your clergyman may say something similar to the following:

Clergyman:

"_____(bride) and _____(groom), the two smaller candles symbolize your individual lives and families. Each of you now take one of the lighted candles and light the unity candle, symbolizing that your individual lives and families are now joined in one light."

V.

SPECIAL CEREMONY ELEMENTS

Now we come to special elements that you may decide to include in your ceremony. To make your ceremony truly unique, personalizing it to the max, you may want to consider one or more of these poignant additions:

- Bell ringers announcing the ceremony
- Honoring your mothers
- Circle of acceptance ceremony
- Family medallion ceremony
- Ceremony of the wishing stones
- Jumping the broom
- Handfasting ceremony
- Covenant of salt or sand
- Memorial tribute
- Communal commitment ceremony
- Renewal of marriage vows by the guests
- Ring church bells or release doves

These precious, meaningful elements are described in the 12 chapters that follow. They are special touches that guests will remember for years to come: "Remember Jim and Cindy's wedding where they included handfasting in their vows?" or "Wasn't that touching when Ashley and Jonathan included their kids in that circle of acceptance ceremony?"

If you want your ceremony to be truly unique and memorable, include one or more of these elements.

Chapter 19

BELL-RINGERS
ANNOUNCING
THE CEREMONY

Bell-ringers are boys or girls of any age who ring crystal or brass bells as they walk up and down the aisles of the church, sanctuary, or other ceremony venue. This bell-ringing takes place immediately prior to the beginning of the ceremony.

Traditionally, the ringing of these bells was thought to ward off evil spirits, but in today's weddings, it's simply a way to let the guests know the ceremony is about to begin. Not only do these bell-ringers add a nice touch to the service, but it's a way to include children in your ceremony who aren't part of the wedding party itself.

If you are including a candle-lighting prelude, the bell-ringing should immediately precede the candle-lighting.

Be sure to add the names of the bell-ringers to your ceremony program, if you have one.

Chapter 20

HONORING
YOUR MOTHERS

It has become a tradition for the bride and/or groom to honor their mothers during their wedding ceremony. They can do so in a variety of ways:

- ∽ After the bride and groom are standing in front of the altar, and just before the wedding ceremony is to begin, they may each walk to their mothers, who are seated, and give them a kiss before returning to their places.

- ∽ In addition to her bouquet, the bride carries two long stemmed roses which she presents to each mother before taking her place beside her groom for the wedding ceremony.

- ∽ Before the bride takes her groom's arm for the recessional, she removes two single flowers from her bridal bouquet, presents the first to her mother with a kiss, the second to the groom's mother with a kiss. The bride then takes her groom's arm for the recessional.

Note: You may honor your grandmothers in a similar manner.

Chapter 21

CIRCLE OF ACCEPTANCE AND FAMILY MEDALLION CEREMONIES

If the bride and/or groom have children from a previous marriage, it's a lovely idea to include them in the ceremony. Two of the most touching ceremonies are the circle of acceptance ceremony and the family medallion ceremony.

Circle of Acceptance Ceremony

This is a sweet ceremony that takes place in front of the altar. You, your children, and the officiant stand in a circle and hold hands. The officiant addresses each child, saying something like this:

Officiant:

"Cindy, your mommy and your new daddy want you to feel accepted into your new family being formed today. They also want your blessing. Do you, Cindy, accept your new family circle?"

Cindy:

"Yes."

Family Medallion Ceremony

The family medallion is a beautiful round medal that has three intertwined circles, symbolizing family, love, and unity. The first two circles represent the union of the man and woman, and the third circle represents the children who are intertwined within their love. The medal is placed on a chain, forming a necklace, which is placed over each child's neck following the couple's wedding vows.

As the parents place the medallions over the necks of their children, they pledge to love and support their children as they become part of their family unit.

The bride and groom each pledge this vow to the children:

"_____and _____ (the first names of their children), today we have become husband and wife, but we have also become a precious new family. I promise to be the best father (or mother) I can possibly be, as I care for you, protect you, support you. and love you with all my heart for all the days of my life."

Chapter 22

ROSE
CEREMONY

A rose ceremony can take place at any wedding venue, whether indoors or outdoors, but it is especially poignant for an outdoor garden ceremony. This ceremony usually follows the recitation of the couple's formal wedding vows, and is introduced by the officiant:

Officiant:

"_____ (bride) and _____ (groom) will now participate in the Ceremony of the Rose. _____(groom) holds a long-stemmed rose that he will present to _____ (bride) and_____ (bride) holds a vase filled with water. The water in the vase symbolizes the protection and nourishment their marriage will provide to each other."

Groom (as he hands his bride a long-stemmed white rose):

"_____, take this rose as a symbol of my love. It began as a tiny bud and blossomed, just as my love has grown and blossomed for you."

Bride (as she places the rose into a bud vase filled with water):

"I take this rose, a symbol of your love, and I place it into water, a symbol of life. For, just as this rose cannot survive without water, I cannot survive without you."

Groom:

"In remembrance of this day, I will give you a white rose each year on our anniversary, as a reaffirmation of my love and the vows spoken here today."

Bride:

"And I will refill this vase with water each year, ready to receive your gift, in reaffirmation of the new life you have given me and the vows spoken here today."

Groom (as he and his bride join hands around the rose-filled vase):

"And so, this rose will be a symbolic memory of my commitment to you this hour; I vow to be a faithful husband to you, to comfort you, honor you, respect you, and cherish you all the days of my life."

Bride (as they continue to hold the vase together):

"And I commit myself to you, to be a faithful wife, to comfort you, honor you, respect you, and cherish you all the days of my life."

Variations of the Rose Ceremony:

- ☙ Following the bride's and groom's rose ceremony, the couple's families also exchange roses during a musical interlude.

- ☙ Following the bride's and groom's rose ceremony, the bride presents a rose to her mother and the groom presents one to his mother.

- ☙ If the bride or groom have children from a previous marriage, each may present a rose to the other's child. For example, the bride may present a rose to her groom's son, and the groom may present a rose to his bride's daughter.

Chapter 23

CEREMONY OF THE WISHING STONES

A wishing stones ceremony, also known as a blessing stones ceremony, may be incorporated into any type of marriage service. There are many variations of this ceremony, but each has the same purpose, casting a good wish or a blessing upon the couple during or after the ceremony.

Stones and note cards are given to each guest as they arrive at the ceremony site. The guests are told that the purpose of these stones and note cards will be explained during the wedding service.

The stones may be gleaming, polished agates, or any other attractive stones. Or, if the wedding is being held outdoors, in a forested area, by a lake or a river, the guests may be asked to gather their own stones from the site before the ceremony begins.

Once each guest has a stone in hand, whether it was given to him or he gathered it from the site, he is asked to write a personalized wedding wish or blessing for the couple on the card. The cards may be preprinted with "helper introductions," such as, "My wish for Jim and Sandy is that _____," or "May Jim and Sandy be blessed with _____."

During the ceremony, the officiant explains the meaning of the wishing stones (or blessing stones) and the personal wishes or blessings each guest is asked to describe on the note cards.

The guests may be asked to read their blessings, or wishes, for the couple as part of the ceremony, or during the wedding reception to follow. In either case, as the guests read off their note cards, they toss their stones into a water-filled container that has been provided for this purpose, placing their note cards in a decorative basket.

The water-filled container becomes a cherished possession that the newlyweds display in a prominent place in their home for all the years to come.

If the ceremony takes place next to a body of water, one variation of this ceremony is for each guest to throw his or her stone into the ocean, lake, or river as each recites his or her wish or blessing for the couple.

Another variation works well for an ocean beach ceremony where, instead of stones, each guest is asked to find a beautiful seashell. The shells are then placed in a container as each guest recites a wish or blessing.

Chapter 24

JUMPING THE BROOM

Jumping the Broom is a meaningful African-American tradition dating back to the 17th century. By jumping over the broom at the end of the ceremony, the bride and groom are symbolizing their love and commitment to each other as they establish a new beginning and a home of their own.

This traditional ritual is usually performed during the ceremony, after the minister pronounces the couple husband and wife.

It may also be performed in a glorious way during the wedding reception. The members of the wedding party precede the bride and groom into the reception venue. Then, just before the couple enters, the broom is laid on the floor in front of them. They jump over the broom as they enter the reception hall, to the applause of their family and friends.

You can purchase a decorated broom, or you can decorate an everyday straw broom in your wedding colors with ribbon and flowers. You may also add small decorations in keeping with your wedding's theme. This broom will be displayed in the couple's home and cherished for all their married life.

Variations include:

- The guests may help decorate the broom prior to the ceremony or reception.

- During the ceremony or reception the guests form a circle around the couple. The couple then uses the broom to sweep around the feet of the guests, as a symbol of sweeping away the old and welcoming the new. Finally, the groom places the broom on the floor, holds his bride's hand, and they jump over the broom as the guests count: "One, two, three... jump!"

- The officiant may pronounce the couple husband and wife after they have jumped the broom, instead of before.

Chapter 25

HANDFASTING
CEREMONIES

Many of today's weddings include a handfasting ceremony. Handfasting, also called "hand tying" or "tying the knot," is often thought of as a Celtic wedding tradition, as seen in the movie *Braveheart*. However, in the movie, instead of tying their wrists together with a cord, the groom's plaid material was used instead.

This handfasting ceremony may take place silently following the pledging of their wedding vows, or the following wording may be used:

Handfasting Vows

Officiant (addressing the guests):

"_____ and _____ have come here today to pledge their vows of marriage."

Officiant (addressing the groom):

"_____, do you take _____(bride) to be your wife? Do you promise to love her, provide for her, and be faithful to her as long as you both shall live?"

Groom:

"I do."

Officiant (addressing the bride):

"_____, do you take _____(groom) to be your husband? Do you promise to love him, honor him, and be faithful to him as long as you both shall live?"

Bride:

"I do."

Officiant (addressing the couple):

"_____ and _____, present your wrists for the handfasting ceremony." (The couple presents their wrists to the officiant.)

Officiant (addressing the couple as he or she ties their wrists together):

"As your wrists are fasted together by this cord (or cloth, plaid, string of cowrie shells, rope, string, braided grass, rosary, etc.), you become bound to each other and to the vows you have promised."

The bride's right wrist is tied to the groom's left wrist. This is symbolic of the couple's commitment and devotion to each other and where the popular phrase originated: "Tying the Knot." Once the bride's and groom's wrists are tied together, the deed is recognized as a binding contract between them and their lives become intertwined for all eternity. In fact, the act of handfasting becomes symbolic of the vows they have taken and their desire to become one.

Handfasting Variations

Traditionally, a silk cord has been used for the handfasting. However, many variations have evolved, including the use of different materials and the way the tying takes place:

- Rope

    A rope is used in many Mexican and Latino ceremonies and is draped in a figure eight over the bride's and groom's shoulders. The draping may be performed by the officiant or by a family member. Or, the draping may be performed by the bride's and groom's godmothers, using a rope with a cross to wrap around the couple's shoulders as the couple kneels at the altar.

∞ *Kente cloth, braided grass, or string of cowrie shells*

In an African-American handfasting ceremony, the couple's hands may be tied together using a strip of Kente cloth, a length of braided grass, or a string of cowrie shells. The couple's hands may be tied by the officiant, a family member, or a close friend.

∞ *String*

A simple string is used to tie the couple's hands together during a Hindu wedding ceremony, in a ritual known as Hasthagranthi.

∞ *Silk fabric or Buddhist rosary*

The bridal couple may include a handfasting ceremony in their Buddhist marriage service. The fabric or rosary (the mala) is gently tied around the wrists of the bride and groom. The tying may be performed by the officiant or by the parents of the couple.

∞ *Prayer stole or shawl*

A Christian couple may use the bride's prayer stole to tie their wrists together, as a symbol of their unity as a married couple, and also of their united faith in God. After the officiant has tied their wrists together with the stole, he or she may also bless the union with the sign of the cross.

Chapter 26

COVENANT OF
SALT OR SAND

This covenant ceremony can be performed using salt or sand. If the wedding takes place on a sandy beach, it's especially meaningful to perform this ceremony using sand. Whether salt or sand is used for this ceremony, however, the meaning is the same.

The bride and groom each hold a container of salt or sand (the salt or sand may be the same color or different colors). The contents of these containers represent their individual lives, with all they were, all they are, and all they will ever be. The bride and groom willingly empty their individual containers of salt or sand into a larger container, symbolizing the joining, or bonding, of their lives for eternity. Just as the grains of salt or sand can never be separated and returned to their individual containers, so the couple is now no longer two, but one, never to be separated one from the other.

Note: If you prefer to use "sentimental" sand for this ceremony, the bride's sand may be from a beach near her home, or the groom's may be from the beach where he asked his bride to marry him. Use your imaginations and you may come up with your own personal supplies of sand.

Vows Recited as Part of the Covenant of Salt or Sand

Officiant:

"For centuries, rings have symbolized the sealing of covenants and commitments."

(The best man gives the bride's ring to the officiant who then holds it up and says:)

"This ring is a circle; it symbolizes the continuity of the marriage bond—a marriage for as long as you both shall live."

(The officiant hands the bride's ring to the groom and instructs him to place it on her finger.)

Officiant (to the groom):

"Do you, _____, give this ring to _____ as a token of your love for her?"

Groom:

"I do."

Officiant:

"Then, as a ceaseless reminder of this hour and of the vows you have taken, _____, place this ring on the hand of your bride and repeat after me:"

Groom (repeating after the minister):

"With this ring I thee wed, with loyal love I thee endow, and all my worldly goods with thee I share, in the name of the Father and the Son and the Holy Spirit. Amen."

(The officiant takes the groom's ring from the maid or matron of honor and holds it up.)

Officiant:

"This ring has not always been the beautiful gold that we see here today. It came from the ground as rough ore—that ore had to be tried by a refiner fire—to drive away the impurities; now only the precious gold remains. May this ring be a symbol of difficult times. Problems will come in your marriage, but they can be like the refiner fire that drives away the impurities—leaving only the precious gold of your love, a love that shall grow more precious and beautiful as years pass by."

(The officiant hands the ring to the bride.)

Officiant (to the bride):

"Do you, _____, give this ring to _____ as an expression of your love for him?"

Bride:

"I do."

Officiant (to the groom):

"Will you, _____, take this ring from _____ as a token of her love for you and will you wear it as an expression of your love for her?"

Groom:

"I will."

Officiant (to the bride):

"Then, as a ceaseless reminder of this hour and of the vows you have taken, _____, place this ring on the hand of your groom and repeat after me."

Bride (repeating after the minister):

"With this ring I thee wed; intreat me not to leave thee or to return from following after thee, for whither thou goest I will go and where thou lodgest I will lodge: thy people shall be my people and thy God my God."

Officiant (to the bride and groom):

"_____ and _____, you have just sealed your covenant by the giving and receiving of rings, and this covenant is a relationship agreement between two parties who agree that they will commit themselves to one another for the keeping of their partnership throughout their lives. The most beautiful example of this partnership is the marriage relationship. You have committed here today to share the rest of your lives with each other and that nothing, save death, will ever cause you to part. You entered this relationship as two distinct individuals, but from this day forth your lives will be so totally melded together that you will never be able to separate. This covenant relationship is symbolized through the pouring of these two individual bags of salt—one representing you, _____, and all that you were, all that you are, and all that you will ever be, and the other representing you, _____ and all that you were and all that you are, and all that you will ever be. As these two bags of salt are poured into the third bag, the individual bags of salt will no longer exist, but will be joined together as one. Just as these grains of salt can never separated and poured again into the individual bags, so will your marriage be. Far more important than your individuality is now the reality that you are no longer two, but one, never to be separated one from the other."

(The bride and groom each empties his or her individual bag of salt into a third bag.)

"_____ and _____, we have heard your vows and you've symbolized your union by pledging your lives to each other, exchanging rings and through the Covenant of Salt (or Sand). So, by the authority of God's word and the state of _____, as a minister of the Gospel, I now pronounce you husband and wife."

Note: Instead of using salt or sand, water may be used. The bride and groom each hold a container of clear or colored water which are poured into one container, signifying a union of two lives that can never be separate again.

Chapter 27

MEMORIAL
TRIBUTE

Memorial tributes have become extremely popular. Here are four examples of tributes that may be included in a wedding ceremony:

- The bride may display a small floral wreath on a stand beside the altar as a tribute to her father who recently passed away.
- The couple may light a special candle in memory of a loved one.
- The bride or groom may carry or wear a memento that belonged to a loved one.
- The groom may include a written tribute to his grandfather in the ceremony program.

The first three examples may also be explained in the ceremony program so that the guests realize the significance of the memorial tribute.

Chapter 28

COMMUNAL COMMITMENT CEREMONY

A communal commitment ceremony is a poignant bonding observance that can be incorporated into any kind of wedding, regardless of its theme. The bonding takes place as the guests and/or family members pledge their commitment to the bride and groom during or after the recitation of their wedding vows. This type of ceremony is especially meaningful for a small wedding attended by the bride's and groom's closest friends and family members.

This is typical vow wording for this type of ceremony:

Officiant:

"_____(groom), are you ready to make the commitment of marriage to _____(bride)?"

Groom:

"Yes, I am."

Officiant:

"_____(bride), are you ready to make the commitment of marriage to _____ (groom)?"

Bride:

I am."

Officiant (addressing the wedding guests):

"Will everyone please stand as we witness _____'s and _____'s wedding vows?"

Officiant asks the groom to repeat after him:

"I,_____, take you, _____, to be my wife, and I promise before God and these witnesses to love you, cherish you, and to keep you special, in plenty and in want, in joy and in sorrow, in sickness and in health, as long as we both shall live."

Officiant asks the bride to repeat after him:

"I,_____, take you, _____, to be my husband, and I promise before God and these witnesses to love you, cherish you, and to keep you special, in plenty and in want, in joy and in sorrow, in sickness and in health, as long as we both shall live."

Officiant addresses the wedding guests:

"Having witnessed _____'s and _____'s wedding vows, will each one of you do everything in your power to uphold _____ and _____ in their marriage? If so, please say, 'we do.'"

Guests:

"We do."

Note:

∞ See the communal commitment vows in Chapter 37. A new life ceremony is for couples where one or both are recovering from addictions, such as to alcohol or drugs. The commitment ceremony in this chapter is especially poignant as the guests and family members vow to love, encourage, and support the couple through all the years of their married life. Candle-lighting is incorporated into this ceremony as well, where all the guests hold their lighted candles high as they pledge their vow of commitment.

∞ Another touching addition to a communal commitment ceremony works well for a small, intimate wedding where only the couple's closest friends and family members are present. The friends and family members form a circle around the couple as they witness their vows and pledge their commitment of support to the couple.

Chapter 29

RENEWAL OF MARRIAGE VOWS BY GUESTS

Following the marriage vows, the clergyman asks all married couples to stand and renew their marriage vows. The clergyman prompts the husbands and wives, as they look into each others' eyes and renew their vows. This is especially touching for a Valentine's Day or New Year's wedding, when the guests are already in a mushy, romantic mood.

Here is sample wording for renewal of marriage vows:

Clergyman (addressing the married guests):

"Couples, please join hands. Gentlemen, please repeat after me:

'I, _____, promise to continue to love, cherish, and protect my wife...to provide for her in health and sickness...to be true to her...and cleave to her until death do us part...I renew my vow to take you, _____, for my wedded wife.'

Ladies, please repeat after me:

'I, _____, promise to continue to love and honor my husband...to be true and faithful to him...and cleave to him until death do us part...I renew my vow to take you, _____, for my wedded husband.'"

Clergyman:

"I do by the virtue of authority vested in me as a minister of the gospel and the authority of the Father, sanction your desire to reaffirm your wedding vows."

Chapter 30

RING CHURCH BELLS
OR RELEASE DOVES

As soon as the ceremony recessional is over, the bride and groom may want to add one or both of these special touches: ring the church bells or release a pair of love doves.

Ring the Church Bells

Immediately following the ceremony, the bride and groom may ring the church bells to announce their marriage to the world, and as a sign of their newfound joy to be husband and wife.

The couple may climb up into a tower to ring the bells by hand, or, if the bells are electronically controlled, the church's custodial staff may ring the bells on cue from the bride and groom.

Release a Pair of Love Doves

The couple may release the doves as they ring the church bells, or they may release them as a uniquely separate action. The doves must be released during the day, however, with enough hours of daylight left for them to fly back to their permanent home.

White doves have traditionally been known as symbols of fidelity, holiness, love, and freedom. The doves may be displayed during the ceremony or reception, or they may be on display inside the entrance of the ceremony venue, for all the guests to see and admire. In any case, when the times comes for the doves to be released, they may be released by hand, as they are lifted into the sky, or they may be released by merely opening the door of their cage or the top of the basket.

In case of bad weather (that prohibits the doves release on the day of the wedding), the doves can at least be displayed as they roost in their cage. Guests are fascinated with these creatures, whether they fly away or not.

VI.

RELIGIOUS CEREMONIES

Religious ceremonies follow certain traditions, depending on the faith. In this section, you'll find chapters that include traditional elements found in the four most common religious ceremonies:

- Jewish ceremony
- Catholic ceremony
- Protestant ceremony
- Interfaith ceremony

V.

RELIGIOUS CEREMONIES

Chapter 31

JEWISH CEREMONY

The Jewish wedding ceremony evolves from both Jewish law and cultural tradition, and is rich in symbolic meaning. The ceremony is usually conducted in both Hebrew and English.

Jewish weddings differ between the Orthodox, Conservative, and Reform branches of the faith. Also, individual rabbis and synagogues within each branch have their own interpretations. For example, depending on the branch of faith, the ceremony may take place in a synagogue, a private home or another indoor or outdoor venue. Also, the ceremony usually may not take place on the Sabbath, on certain holy days, or during some seasons of the year. However, a ceremony usually may take place on the Sabbath or on a festival day if scheduled at least an hour after sunset.

Jewish traditions also apply to wedding attire. For example, an Orthodox Jewish bride is required to wear a long sleeved gown, and all branches of the faith observe customs regarding the bride's veil. The only requirement for the groom, and this is observed in all branches of the Jewish faith, is that he must wear a yarmulke (a prayer skull cap).

Consult with your rabbi regarding his interpretations and directives regarding all elements of the ceremony.

You'll find that he will become, not only your best resource as you plan your ceremony, but a caring friend.

Typical Order of Service for a Jewish Ceremony

A Jewish wedding ceremony is usually only 20 minutes long and consists of:

- Processional
- The bride, groom, their attendants, and families gather under the chuppah
- Invocation by the rabbi
- Blessings of betrothal (birkat erusin): The bride and groom receive these blessings from the rabbi as they sip a ceremonial wine
- Wedding vows are recited
- Ring vows are recited
- The ketubah is read aloud
- Seven friends or family members read the seven blessings, during which time the bride and groom sip ceremonial wine from the kiddush cups
- Groom breaks a glass with his foot (the bride may also participate in this ritual)
- Benediction by the rabbi
- Recessional

Elements Common to Jewish Weddings

The following are elements common to Jewish weddings, many of which date back centuries:

Mikveh (Ritual Bath)

A day or so before the wedding, the bride is cleansed in a ritual bath, called the Mikveh. This allows her to enter marriage in a pure state. Before her ritual bath, she must remove all rings, hair accessories, bandages, and nail polish, to assure there is no barrier between her body and the cleansing bath.

Ufruf (Reading of the Torah)

This is a ritual practiced by Orthodox and Conservative Jews where the groom reads from the Torah and recites the proper blessings over it. The rabbi then has the bride join the groom and he blesses them both for their forthcoming marriage.

Processional

This is a suggested order for your processional:

- ∞ The chuppah carried by four chuppah holders (if not using a freestanding chuppah)
- ∞ Rabbi
- ∞ Cantor
- ∞ Grandparents, who are ushered to their seats
- ∞ Ring bearer and flower girl
- ∞ Male and female members of the wedding party walk in pairs, men on the left and women on the right
- ∞ Maid or matron of honor
- ∞ Best man (or may walk beside the maid or matron of honor, on her left)
- ∞ Groom (flanked by his parents)
- ∞ Bride (flanked by her parents)*

* This is practiced by Orthodox and some Conservative Jews. Reform Jews and other Conservative Jews have modified this custom so that only the bride's father walks her down the aisle.

The parents kiss their child before entering the chuppah. The groom escorts his bride into the chuppah, where she stands to his right. If it is an Orthodox ceremony, the bride circles her groom seven times, representing the seven wedding blessings. Depending on the interpretation of your rabbi, the bride and groom may stand close to each other under the chuppah, holding hands or with arms around each other's waists. If one of you wears a tallith, share it with the other by pulling it over his or her shoulder.

The groom's parents stand beside their son, and the bride's parents stand beside their daughter. The best man stands next to the left front pole of the chuppah, and the bride's honor attendant stands next to the right front pole. The remaining attendants may either stand in front of the chuppah, facing the congregation, or ring the back of the chuppah.

Note: You may use processional music of your choice. However, any music composed by Mendelssohn or Wagner is not acceptable because it has been said they were anti-Semite. Look through the popular processional music selections in Chapter 7. Once you've made your selection, check with your rabbi to be sure it is acceptable.

Chuppah

The chuppah (pronounced hoopah) is a wedding canopy placed in the front of the venue. If you're being married in a synagogue, you will be provided with a chuppah. Otherwise, a chuppah may be rented, or you can make your own. It is made from fabric whose four corners are attached to the top of four poles. A floral or velvet fabric is often used, with optional embroidery and fringes.

The chuppah symbolizes God's presence and the couple's new home. A tallith, also known as a prayer shawl, may be used instead of fabric. It is rectangular in shape, with four tzitzit (fringes) on each corner. Depending on the branch of Jewish faith, the chuppah may also be decorated with ribbons and flowers.

Standing under the chuppah should be a small table to hold the ceremonial wine, the kiddush cups, decanter, and the glasses to smash.

Ceremonial Wine

The ceremonial wine should be kosher. It may be poured into a decanter prior to the service, which provides formal service, as opposed to serving from the wine bottle. The wine is poured into kiddush cups for the two wine blessings. The first blessing is symbolic of the commitment of the betrothal; the second blessing is symbolic of the commitment of marriage.

Vows

No single set of rules applies to all Jewish wedding vow phrasings, because of the differences between the Orthodox, Conservative, and Reform branches of the faith. In the Orthodox and Conservative wedding services, an ancient Aramaic vow is usually recited before the groom places the ring on his bride's finger. This ring vow also serves as the groom's wedding vow. In the Sephardic transliteration, it reads:

"Harey at mekuddeshet li B'taba'at zo k'dat Moshe V'israel"

which means:

"Behold thou are consecrated unto me with this ring according to the law of Moses and of Israel."

In a double-ring ceremony, the bride presents a ring to her groom in the same way, reciting a slightly different vow.

For a Conservative service, these vows are often used, as taken from the *Rabbinical Assembly Manual* and published by the Rabbinical Assembly of America (1999):

Rabbi (addressing the bridegroom):

"Do you, _____, take _____ to be your lawful wedded wife, to love, to honor, and to cherish?"

Bridegroom:

"I do."

Rabbi (addressing the bride):

"Do you, _____, take _____ to be your lawful wedded husband to love, to honor, and to cherish?"

Bride:

"I do."

Rabbi (addressing the bridegroom):

"Then, _____, put this ring upon the finger of your bride and say to her: 'Be thou consecrated to me, as my wife, by this ring, according to the Law of Moses and of Israel.'"

The rabbi then asks the bride to repeat the following:

"May this ring I receive from thee be a token of my having become thy wife according to the Law of Moses and of Israel."

If two rings are used, the bride may say:

"This ring is a symbol that thou art my husband in accordance with the Law of Moses and Israel."

In a Reformed service there is a distinctly separate wedding vow that is read by the rabbi and affirmed by the bride and groom:

"O God, supremely blessed, supreme in might and glory, guide and bless this groom and bride. Standing here in the presence of God, the guardian of the home, ready to enter into the bond of wedlock, answer in the fear of God, and in the hearing of those assembled:

Do you, _____, of your own free will and consent take _____ to be your wife/husband and do you promise to love, honor, and cherish her/him throughout life?"

Groom/bride:

"I do."

Rabbi (addressing the bridegroom):

"Do you, _____, take _____ to be your lawful wedded wife, to love, to honor, and to cherish?"

Bridegroom:

"I do."

Rabbi (addressing the bride):

"Do you, _____, take _____ to be your lawful wedded husband to love, to honor, and to cherish?"

Bride:

"I do."

Giving of the Ring

The ring is usually a plain gold band, with no engravings or inset stones. It belongs to the groom who gives it to his bride as he recites a traditional vow of acquisition and consecration. He places it on his bride's right index finger, which is traditionally known as the finger of intelligence, because it is the finger that points at the words while reading the Torah. (Modern brides switch the ring to the left hand after the ceremony.) By accepting this ring, she becomes his wife, thus fulfilling the ancient Jewish custom of accepting an object worth more than a dime from the groom.

Rabbi (addressing the bridegroom):

"Then, _____, put this ring upon the finger of your bride and say to her: 'Be thou consecrated to me, as my wife, by this ring, according to the Law of Moses and of Israel."

The rabbi then asks the bride to repeat the following:

"May this ring I receive from thee be a token of my having become thy wife according to the Law of Moses and of Israel."

If two rings are used, the bride may say:

"This ring is a symbol that thou art my husband in accordance with the Law of Moses and Israel."

Ketubah

The ketubah is a beautiful and elaborate document which is usually signed immediately prior to the ceremony and presented during the ceremony itself. It is a religious marriage document that sets the terms of the marriage. It may be Reform, Conservative, or Orthodox, preprinted or personalized with your choice of artwork and various text.

Traditionally, the ketubah was signed only by the groom, but according to modern Jewish customs, it is also signed by the bride. After signing the ketubah, it is traditional for the groom to go up to his bride, lift her veil, and gaze into her eyes, confirming that she is the woman he has chosen to marry. This ritual is known as a bedeken, representing the lesson learned from the story of Jacob who was tricked into marrying a woman other than the one he wanted to marry.

This precious document should be signed in the presence of two witnesses, neither one of whom can be related to bride or groom. If your ketubah is quite large, it may be displayed on an easel during the ceremony. Guard this document and keep it safe because you may wish to display it in your home.

The ketubah is read during the wedding ceremony. It is then presented by the groom to his bride, who hands it to her maid or matron of honor for safekeeping.

Reading or a Poem

If you would like to have a certain reading or poem included in your ceremony, show it to your rabbi first to be sure it's acceptable to him. Also, ask him where he suggests it be placed within your ceremony.

The Seven Blessings (Sheva b'rachot)

The seven blessings may be read by one family member, or by seven family members, one blessing each:

"You Abound in Blessings, Adonai our God, who created the fruit of the vine.

"You Abound in Blessings, Adonai our God. You created all things for Your glory.

"You Abound in Blessings, Adonai our God. You created humanity.

"You Abound in Blessings, Adonai our God. You made humankind in Your image, after Your likeness, and You prepared from us a perpetual relationship. You abound in Blessings, Adonai our God. You created humanity.

"May she who was barren rejoice when her children are united in her midst in joy. You Abound in Blessings, Adonai our God, who makes Zion rejoice with her children.

"You make these beloved companions greatly rejoice even as You rejoiced in Your creation in the Garden of Eden as of old. You Abound in Blessings, Adonai our God, who makes the bridegroom and bride to rejoice.

"You Abound in Blessings, Adonai our God, who created joy and gladness, bridegroom and bride, mirth and exultation, pleasure and delight, love, fellowship, peace, and friendship. Soon may there be heard in the cities of Judah and in the streets of Jerusalem, the voice of joy and gladness, the voice of the bridegroom and the voice of the bride, the jubilant voice of bridegrooms from their canopies and of youths from their feasts of song. You Abound in Blessings, Adonai our God. You make the bridegroom rejoice with the bride."

Breaking of the Glass

At the end of the ceremony, the groom stomps on the glass, which has been wrapped in a cloth, shattering it into many pieces. If the bride also participates in this ritual, it is preferable to use a delicate champagne flute, which breaks easily. This breaking of the glass is symbolic of several things:

- ∞ The destruction of the temple of Jerusalem
- ∞ That the marriage is an irrevocable act, as permanent and final as the broken glass is irreparable
- ∞ A warning of the frailty of marriage and how it should be handled with care, being careful not to crush it or break it

Benediction by the Rabbi

The rabbi recites this blessing over the new husband and wife:

"May the Lord bless you and protect you. May the Lord show you favor and be gracious to you. May the Lord turn in loving kindness to you and grant you peace.

Amen."

Recessional

This is a suggested order for your recessional:

- Bride and groom
- Bride's parents
- Groom's parents
- Maid or matron of honor on the arm of the best man
- Male and female members of the wedding party, walking in pairs
- Ring bearer and flower girl, walking side by side
- Cantor
- Rabbi
- The chuppah carried by four chuppah holders (if not using a freestanding chuppah)

Note: You may have recessional music of your choice. However, just as with the processional music, any music composed by Mendelssohn or Wagner is not acceptable. Look through the popular recessional music selections in Chapter 14. Once you've made your selection, check with your rabbi to be sure it is acceptable.

Yichud

It is a Jewish tradition for the bride and groom to have a special, quiet time together immediately following the ceremony. Ask your caterer to leave two plates of food for you beforehand so that you may eat your first meal together in private, breaking your fast, if applicable. This yichud should take place in a room that can be locked for total privacy.

Note: If you are planning an interfaith Jewish ceremony, see Chapter 34.

Chapter 32

CATHOLIC CEREMONY

The Catholic Church in America, also called the Roman Catholic Church, or the Church of Rome, follows strict doctrinal traditions, including those pertaining to the marriage ceremony. The marriage ceremony, also called the Nuptial Rite, may take place with or without a mass. If a mass is included, the service resembles a regular Sunday service with a wedding incorporated into it. Although adherence to traditions may vary slightly according to each individual parish priest's interpretation, there is usually very little deviation from tradition. This is especially true when the vows are recited during a wedding mass, which always includes the Eucharist, also called Communion.

Two examples of a Catholic wedding follow; the first includes a mass, and the second does not.

Catholic Wedding With a Mass

- ∞ Introductory rite
- ∞ Processional
- ∞ Greeting (optional)
- ∞ Gathering song (optional if processional hymn was sung)

- Penitential rite
- Opening prayer
- Liturgy of the Word
- First reading (from Old Testament)
- Responsorial Psalm (may be sung by a cantor or recited)
- Second reading (from New Testament)
- Gospel acclamation
- Gospel reading
- Homily
- Rite of Marriage

> The priest asks the bride and groom questions regarding their faithfulness to each other, freedom of choice, acceptance of and upbringing of children.

- Exchange of consent (the wedding vows)

> Here are two generally acceptable vow phrasings included in a nuptial mass:

> "I, _____, take you, _____, for my lawful wife/husband, to have and to hold, from this day forward, for better, for worse, for richer, for poorer, in sickness and health, until death do us part."

or

> "I,_____, take you, _____, to be my husband/wife. I promise to be true to you in good times and in bad, in sickness and in health. I will love and honor you all the days of my life."

- Blessing of the rings
- Exchange of the rings
- General Intercessions
- Liturgy of the Eucharist (Communion)

- Presentation of the gifts and preparation of the altar
- Eucharist prayer
- Sanctus
- Memorial acclamation
- Great amen

  (The last three elements are usually sung)
- Communion rite
- Lord's prayer
- Nuptial blessing
- Sign of peace
- Agnus Dei (usually sung)
- Communion hymn
- Concluding rite
- Final blessing
- Dismissal
- Introduction of married couple and the kiss
- Recessional

A Catholic bride often includes the honoring of the Virgin Mary during the Nuptial Mass. She may honor her by including the song Ave Maria, which may be played or sung by a soloist during the Prelude; or, she may include a special prayer, such as Hail, Holy Queen. Another poignant option is to present all or part of her bridal bouquet at the foot of the statue of the Virgin Mary. This takes place before she and her groom walk back down the aisle as a married couple.

Catholic Wedding Without a Mass

- Entrance Rite
- Processional
- Liturgy of the Word
- Homily

- Rite of Marriage
- General intercessions
- Lord's prayer
- Final Blessings

Depending on the traditions of their particular parish, the bridal couple should meet with their priest who may allow them to make certain changes or additions to their ceremony, including:

- The order of their Processional and/or Recessional (see the following paragraph)
- Personalized wedding vows
- Choice of scriptural readings
- Choice of readings
- Choice of music
- Choice of prayers
- Incorporating a Unity Candle ceremony into the service
- Adding a memorial candle

Note: A Papal Blessing, a special blessing directly from the Pope, may be obtained for your ceremony. Contact the Chancery Office of your diocese who will provide you with the application, which should be submitted as soon as you've set the date and place for your wedding. The blessing is recorded on parchment paper that includes the Pope's official raised seal, signature, and blessing.

Traditional Order for a Catholic Processional and Recessional

Unless the bride and groom receive permission from the priest to change the orders, these are the traditional orders for a Catholic processional and recessional:

Processional

This is a suggested order for your processional (the priest, groom, and best man wait at the altar):

- The groomsmen escort the bridesmaids down the aisle, beginning with the groomsman and bridesmaid who will stand farthest from the bride and groom
- Ring bearer
- Flower girl
- Maid/matron of honor
- Bride escorted by her father (or other close male family member) on his left side

Two acceptable options:

- The priest welcomes the bride and groom and their families at the entrance to the church. He then leads the couple and their families to the altar.
- The groomsmen may enter from the side with the priest, groom, and best man, in which case the bridesmaids walk down the aisle single file.

Recessional

The recessional is in this order:

- Bride and groom
- Flower girl and ring bearer (optional)
- Honor attendants (maid/matron of honor and best man)

Chapter 33

PROTESTANT
CEREMONY

Protestant ceremonies vary greatly, depending not only on their degree of formality, but, more importantly, the customs of each denomination. This chapter contains an example of a typical Protestant marriage service.

Typical Protestant Ceremony

This sample ceremony will give you a general idea of the elements and order of a typical Protestant wedding ceremony.

Candle-lighting Prelude

Six girls, wearing matching gowns similar to the bridesmaids,' enter the ceremony venue from the rear. Three girls slowly proceed down each side, lighting any candles that have been mounted in sconces on the pillars and in candelabra standing behind the altar. During this candle-lighting prelude, a pianist plays *Air from Water Music*, by Handel. After lighting the candles, the girls move to the far left and right of the altar area as the clergyman, the groom, his best man, and groomsmen enter from a side door and stand on the right side of the venue, facing the groom's family and friends.

Processional

- The bridesmaids enter the venue from the rear, walking slowly down the aisle, accompanied by the organ playing Romance from *Eine Kleine Nachtmusik* by Mozart.

- They are followed by the bride's maid of honor, the flower girl, and then the ring bearer.

- The bride's mother stands and faces the rear of the venue as the organ begins playing the Wedding March from *Lohengrin* (Here Comes the Bride) by Wagner.

- The bride is walked down the aisle on her father's left arm. When they reach the altar, the clergyman asks, "Who gives this woman to be married to this man?" Her father answers, "Her mother and I do." Her father puts his daughter's hand into the groom's and then is seated next to the bride's mother.

Convocation / Invocation

Clergyman:

"We are gathered here today in the presence of these witnesses to join _____ (bride) and _____(groom) in holy matrimony, which is commended to be honorable among all men and to be entered into reverently and discreetly.

"God, our Father in heaven, the source of all love, please be present today during this sacred ceremony. We especially ask your blessing on this couple, who stands before us, and for all of us who share their joy. May each one of us sense your love and may we be filled with your love as we witness the vows of _____(bride) and _____(groom). Amen."

Reading

The groom's aunt reads this scripture from the book of Ruth in the Bible:

> "Entreat me not to leave thee,
> Or to return from following after thee:
> For wither thou goest, I will go,
> And where thou lodgest, I will lodge.
> Thy people shall be my people,
> And thy God my God.
> Where thou diest, will I die,
> And there will I be buried.
> The Lord do so to me, and more also,
> If ought but death part thee and me."
> —Ruth 1:16–17

Musical Selection

A friend of the bride sings Morning Has Broken (by Eleanor Farjeon).

Address or Homily

Clergyman (addressing the bride and groom):

"We are here today because of a miracle, the miracle of your love _____(bride) and _____(groom). Marriage was established by God, our Father, as we read in Chapter 2 of the book of Genesis:

"And the Lord God caused a deep sleep to fall upon Adam, and he slept: and he took one of his ribs, and closed up the flesh instead thereof; and the rib, which the Lord God had taken from man, made he a woman, and brought her unto the man. And Adam said,

'This is now bone of my bones, and flesh of my flesh: she shall be called Woman, because she was taken out of Man. Therefore shall a man leave his father and his mother and shall cleave unto his wife: and they shall be one flesh.'

"God didn't form Eve from Adam's foot, that he may stomp on her, or from his head, that he may rule over her, but from his side, that she may be his helpmate and companion.

"I know that your deep abiding love for each other comes from God above, for God is love, and your love is to be nurtured, cherished, and expanded every day as you draw closer to each other and closer to God. For marriage is not merely the act of living together and pleasing each other, but of living for God and pleasing Him.

"May you be each other's comfort and strength, as God guards and protects you all the days of your life. Listen to each other, encourage each other, respect each other and stand by each other's side as you walk together as husband and wife. Put God first in your marriage, always seeking His will, as you abide in love, just as the love chapter describes:

'Love is patient, love is kind. It does not envy, it does not boast, it is not proud. It is not rude, it is not self-seeking, it is not easily angered, it keeps no record of wrongs. Love does not delight in evil, but rejoices with the truth. It always protects, always hopes, always perseveres. Where there are prophecies, they will cease; where there are tongues, they will be stilled; where there is knowledge, it will pass away, but love never fails. And now these three remain: Faith, Hope, and Love, but the greatest of these is Love.'

"My prayer for you, and I'm sure the prayers of your friends and family assembled here today, is that your marriage will always be beautiful. Always new. May it be protected by God's love, and may no one ever disturb your holy union. God bless you both."

Consecration and Expression of Intent

(Delivered by the Clergyman)

"Our holy God, please sanctify the marriage vows to be spoken today by _____(bride) and _____(groom). As their vows are spoken, may they not only dedicate themselves to each other, but to you for the sacred purpose of serving you as a married couple.

Clergyman (to the bride):

"_____, is it your intent to marry _____ today? To bond to him as his wife?"

Bride: "Yes."

Clergyman (to the groom):

"_____, is it your intent to marry _____today? To bond to her as her husband?"

Groom: "Yes."

Vows

(The clergyman asks the bride and groom to repeat the following)

"I,_____, take thee, _____, to be my wedded husband/wife, to have and to hold from this day forward, for better, for worse, for richer, for poorer, in sickness and in health, to love and to cherish, till death do us part, according to God's holy ordinance; and thereto I plight/give thee my troth."

Ring Exchange

Clergyman (to the bride and groom):

"I will ask you now to seal the vows which you have just made by the giving and receiving of rings. Let us remember that the circle is the emblem of eternity and it is our prayer that your love and happiness will be as unending as the rings which you exchange."

Clergyman (to the groom):

"_____, do you have a token of your love?"

Groom: "Yes, a ring."

(The best man gives the ring to the minister; the minister gives it to the groom; the groom places it on his bride's finger and then repeats after the minister:)

"This ring I give thee, in token and pledge, of our constant faith, and abiding love."

Clergyman (to the bride):

"_____, do you have a token of your love?"

Bride:

"Yes, a ring."

(The maid/matron of honor gives the ring to the clergyman; the clergyman gives it to the bride; the bride places it on her groom's finger and then repeats after the clergyman):

"This ring I give thee, in token and pledge, of our constant faith, and abiding love."

Lighting of the Unity Candle

The bride and groom walk together to the unity candle (a large candle that sits unlighted between two smaller lighted candles that represent the families of the bride and groom). The bride and groom each lift one of the smaller candles and, together, light the larger unity candle as the clergyman says:

"_____(bride) and _____(groom), the two smaller candles symbolize your individual lives and families. Each of you now take one of the lighted candles and light the unity candle, symbolizing that your individual lives and families are now joined as one."

The couple blows their individual candles out and then returns to their place in front of the altar.

Pronouncement and Kiss

Clergyman:

"May you keep this covenant you have made. May you bless each other in your marriage, comforting each other when one needs comfort, sharing each other's joys when one needs someone to share it, and helping each other in all your endeavors throughout your married lives together. And now, by the power vested in me by the laws of the state of Idaho, I pronounce you husband and wife."

Clergyman (to the groom):

"You may kiss your bride."

Benediction

Clergyman:

Dear God, bless _____ and _____ as they leave this place, and bless their family and friends who have come here to share in this great day. May the Lord go with you all."

Clergyman, to the congregation:

"May I present to you Mr. and Mrs. _____."

Honoring the Mothers

Before the bride takes her groom's arm for the recessional, she removes two single flowers from her bridal bouquet, presents the first to her mother with a kiss, the second to the groom's mother with a kiss. The bride then takes her groom's arm for the recessional.

Recessional

The recessional takes place in this order, accompanied by the organ playing La Rejouissance from *Royal Fireworks Music* by Handel:

- Bride and groom
- Maid of honor on the arm of the best man
- The bridesmaids, each on the arm of a groomsman
- The flower girl and ring bearer walking side by side
- The candle-lighters, walking in pairs

Note: See Chapters 10 and 11 for wedding and ring vows common to other Protestant denominations.

Chapter 34

INTERFAITH CEREMONIES

Interfaith weddings have become commonplace. An interfaith service may be conducted by a clergyperson sympathetic to the individual faiths of the bride and groom, or the service may be purely ecumenical with two officiants, one representing the bride, and one the groom.

In some cases it isn't possible for an interfaith marriage to be officially sanctioned at all, especially if the bride or groom was married before, or if the bride or groom comes from a religious background with strict regulations against interfaith marriages. In cases such as these, the couple will usually compromise in one of these ways:

- The bride or groom converts to the other's faith
- Have a civil (secular) ceremony, conducted by an officiant legally sanctioned to conduct marriages in their state

Orthodox and Conservative Jewish rabbis, for example, usually refuse to officiate at a mixed marriage and the Roman Catholic attitude is usually that, on a case-by-case basis, it may be possible for a Catholic to marry a non-Catholic, but only under certain conditions. For example, in such a marriage a Catholic groom may be required to promise, either in writing or orally, that he will do all in his power to share the Catholic faith with any children that may result from the union; he must also promise that these children will be baptized and reared as Catholics.

There are multitudes of rules and restrictions within Protestant denominations as well. These rules not only vary from one denomination to the other, but from one congregation to another. For example, a divorced person usually may not be married within the Episcopal faith, except by special permission, and in order for a couple to be married in a Quaker wedding service, at least one of the couple must be a member of the Religious Society of Friends. The restrictions are so varied that it's always wise to set an appointment with the clergyperson of the particular church you have chosen before making further plans.

Jew Marrying a Non-Jew

It is very difficult to find a rabbi who will conduct a wedding ceremony for a Jew and a non-Jew. Orthodox and Conservative rabbis will never conduct such a ceremony, and only a minute percentage of Reform rabbis will do so. One reason for this policy is that one of the most important purposes of a Jewish ceremony is to establish and consecrate a Jewish family. This would obviously not be possible for a Jew married to a non-Jew.

Compromises:

∞ The non-Jew converts to the Jewish faith

∞ The Jew and non-Jew find a rabbi willing to marry them in a modified Jewish ceremony where certain traditional Jewish liturgical phrasings are deleted. If this ceremony is conducted by a Reform rabbi, he will not agree to co-officiate the ceremony with a clergyman of a non-Jewish faith.

∞ The Jew and non-Jew marry in a civil ceremony, conducted by a secular officiant, such as a judge or justice of the peace. The ceremony venue may be any non-religious setting, such as a hotel ballroom, a home, or a rose garden. This type of ceremony allows great freedom for both the bride and groom to include any Jewish or non-Jewish symbols they choose, including readings from the Old and New Testament. If a Jew is marrying a Christian, for example, these are popular vow phrasings that may be used:

"I, _____, take you, _____, to be my wedded wife/husband; and I promise and covenant, before God and these witnesses, to be your loving and faithful husband/wife, in plenty and in want, in joy and in sorrow, in sickness and in health, as long as we both shall live."

Or this simpler version may also be used:

Officiant to the Bride/Groom:

"Do you, _____, take _____ to be your lawfully wedded wife/husband, and do you promise to love, honor, and cherish her/him as long as you shall live/love?"

Bride/Groom:

"I do."

Catholic Marrying a Non-Catholic

The wedding of a Catholic and a non-Catholic usually includes one of these vows:

"I, _____, take you, _____, to be my wife/husband. I promise to be true to you in good times and in bad, in sickness and in health. I will love you and honor you all the days of my life."

or

The Priest to the Groom/Bride:

"_____, do you take _____ to be your wife/husband? Do you promise to be true to her/him in good times and in bad, in sickness and in health, to love him/her and honor him/her all the days of your life?"

Groom/Bride:

"I do."

Catholic Marrying a Jew

This type of wedding service is usually co-officiated by a priest and a rabbi and the wedding vows vary; consisting of an Introduction by the priest or rabbi. The bride and groom compose their own vows or incorporate phrasings from the traditional Catholic and Jewish services. A common alternative is as follows:

"_____, I accept you as my wife/husband and call upon the Jewish and Christian communities to witness our union."

VII.

ELEMENTS OF OTHER POPULAR CEREMONIES

Other ceremonies are also popular for today's couples and their unique elements are included in this section:

- ∞ Civil ceremony
- ∞ Encore ceremony
- ∞ New life ceremony
- ∞ Nature ceremony

The traditional civil ceremony model has been common for many years, especially for the couple getting married at the county courthouse. The rest of the ceremonies described in this section have become popular within the last decade or so.

Chapter 35

CIVIL
CEREMONY

A civil, or secular marriage is a legal contract that conveys all the rights and responsibilities of marriage, compared to a religious ceremony that is also a spiritual pronouncement of the union of a husband wife. A civil wedding meets the state's requirements for a legal marriage. In other words, the marriage will be recognized in the eyes of the law, especially when it comes to ownership or exchange of property.

Your civil wedding ceremony may be formal or informal, long or short, and it may be held in any secular setting, such as the judge's chambers, a hotel ballroom, a private home, on a beach, on top of a mountain, in a beautiful garden, on a boat, in a restaurant, or at any non-religious venue.

How to Arrange a Civil Wedding

🚩 Locate a licensed official authorized by your state to perform weddings, such as a mayor, city clerk, court clerk, justice, judge, or a civic marriage officer. You can do this by calling the office of your local marriage bureau, which will provide you with their telephone numbers.

- ∞ Meet with this officiant to see if he or she is available to perform the ceremony on the date and time of your wedding.

- ∞ Discuss the officiant's fee. Ask if an additional fee applies for the officiant to travel to your ceremony venue. This factor is important to settle in advance, because some charge a set fee, while others accept only a gratuity.

- ∞ Ask to see copies of sample ceremonies used by the officiant. Review them and discuss any changes or additions you would like to make, if allowable.

- ∞ Discuss what the officiant will wear, if other than a judicial robe.

- ∞ If your wedding will be held at a venue other than the courthouse or judge's chambers, will the officiant be available to attend your wedding rehearsal?

- ∞ Ask the officiant if he or she has any special preferences or requirements.

Contact your marriage license bureau or your local municipal clerk as soon as you become engaged so that you can be aware of the requirements:

- ∞ When can you apply for your marriage license?

- ∞ How long is the license valid?

- ∞ Is there a waiting period between the time of application and the wedding?

- ∞ What is the fee?

ᢒ Which documents should we bring with us when we apply? (Such as, identification, proof of age, copy of divorce decree from a previous marriage, if applicable.)

ᢒ Is a blood test required? What are the time requirements for obtaining the tests?

Note: Does your county or state allow a friend or relative to be authorized to perform your ceremony? Many do, which means that you can have your own personal officiant to marry you. This type of special license is usually a one day only license which gives him or her the power to marry you on your wedding day.

Typical Courthouse Civil Ceremony

If your wedding will be held in a courthouse, your ceremony will be brief and your wedding party will be small. You'll probably only have in attendance your best man, maid or matron of honor, your parents, and siblings. Each officiant has his or her own standard wording for a civil ceremony. However, here is typical wording for such a ceremony:

Judge (or other legal officiant):

"We are gathered here today to unite _____(bride) and _____(groom) in marriage. Those who enter into this relationship must honor their vows and be faithful to each other in all circumstances: whether in sickness or health, sorrow or joy, in poverty or prosperity."

Judge (addressing the groom):

"_____, will you have this woman to be your wife in good times and bad, in joy and in sorrow, in sickness and in health, as long as you both shall live? If so, answer, I will."

Groom:

"I will."

Judge (addressing the bride):

"_____, will you have this man to be your husband, in good times and bad, in joy and in sorrow, in sickness and in health, as long as you both shall live? If so, answer, I will."

Bride:

"I will."

Groom (addressing his bride, with prompting by the judge):

"I, _____, take thee _____ to be my wedded spouse, and I do promise before these witnesses to be thy loving and faithful spouse, in good times and bad, in joy and in sorrow, in sickness and in health, as long as we both shall live."

Bride (addressing her groom, with prompting by the judge):

"I, _____, take thee _____ to be my wedded spouse, and I do promise before these witnesses to be thy loving and faithful spouse, in good times and bad, in joy and in sorrow, in sickness and in health, as long as we both shall live."

Judge:

"Do you wish to exchange rings?"

Bride and groom:

"Yes."

Groom (to his bride with prompting by the judge):

"This ring I give you, in token and in pledge, of our constant faith and abiding love."

Bride (to her groom with prompting by the judge):

"This ring I give you, in token and in pledge, of our constant faith and abiding love."

Judge:

"May the love and joy you both feel today continue forever. And now by the authority committed unto me, according to the law of the State of _____, I declare that _____ and _____ are now husband and wife."

Judge (addressing the groom):

"You may now kiss your bride."

Note: Many civil officiants offer the bride and groom a choice of ceremony phrasings, usually printed in a booklet the couple may consider ahead of time. Also, some of these officiants allow the bride and groom to write their own marriage and ring vows, although they must be reviewed and approved before the ceremony.

Chapter 36

Encore
Ceremony

An encore ceremony is one where the bride, the groom, or both have been married before. The ceremony may be large or small, elaborate or modest. The choice is up to you. If this is the first marriage for one of you, you may wish to have a fullblown affair, especially if it's the bride's first wedding.

Common Elements Found in Encore Weddings

Encore weddings tend to have these commonalties:

- Usually smaller and less elaborate than the first
- Great emphasis on the importance and sanctity of their commitment to each other
- Total cost of the wedding is about $10,000 less than a first wedding
- The couple spends more on the honeymoon than on the wedding
- If the first marriage ended in pain or bitterness, the bride or groom wants the encore wedding to be as different as possible from their first

- The bride may wear any color gown, including white; however, the gown will usually not have a long train, and the veil (if there is one) does not cover her face
- Bride and groom write their own personalized wedding vows
- Personalized vows composed especially for each child
- Include their children in the ceremony

Personalized Vows for an Encore Ceremony

An encore wedding takes on a serious tone, as the couple realizes the importance and sanctity of the ceremony, including their vows. Here are several examples of encore wedding vows taken from my book, *Diane Warner's Complete Book of Wedding Vows, 2nd Edition*, (2006, New Page Books):

"_____, you are my new day, a beautiful ray of light that broke through the darkness of my despair. I thank God for sending you to me with your smile, your sense of humor, and your loving spirit. I take you today as my wedded wife/husband, and I promise to love you and cherish you all the days of my life."

*****

"_____, you are my healer, my comforter, and the joy of my life. Your love has restored my torn, broken heart; your smile has healed my pain; and your caring spirit has rescued mine from the dark places. I love you, _____, and I vow to be a faithful, loving husband/wife, to care for you, to comfort you and to cherish you for as long as we both shall live."

*****

"I,_____, take you, _____, as my lawfully wedded husband/wife. I promise to love you and be true to you in sickness and in health, in good times and bad, always putting you first in my life. I thank God for rescuing me from my despair by sending you to me, my cherished treasure, His most precious, undeserved gift."

*****

"_____, I thank God for you and for the joyous light and peace you have brought to me at a dark time in my life. With a love that will never falter and our abiding faith in one another, I vow to take you, _____, as my husband/wife, to love you, honor you, and cherish you now and forevermore, so help me God."

*****

"As we begin our new life together as husband and wife, I am amazed at our love. It is an invisible thing—our love—and yet, it is a force so strong, so durable that it will hold our lives together for all the years to come. Our past is over; our future is new, and as we take our vows today, we will be changed forever, and I take them gladly, and without reservation. _____, I commit myself to you, to be your loving, faithful husband/wife. I promise to honor you, believe in you, protect you and do everything in my power to make your life happy and fulfilled. This is my promise. Take my hand as we go with joy into our new life together."

Ways to Include Your Children in the Ceremony

Your children should feel part of the ceremony, so much so that in years to come they will remember it as the "day we got married." Here are several ways you can include your children:

Include Them in Your Wedding

Your children may serve as:

- ∞ Best man
- ∞ Maid of honor
- ∞ Flower girl
- ∞ Ring bearer
- ∞ Bell-ringers
- ∞ Candle-lighters
- ∞ Usher
- ∞ Walk you down the aisle
- ∞ Read a poem or special verse
- ∞ Hand out wedding programs
- ∞ Sing a song
- ∞ Perform on a musical instrument

Order flowers for all your children, including a boutonniere for your young son or a small wrist corsage for your young daughter.

Include Them in Your Vows

Sixty-four percent of encore wedding couples have children from previous marriages, so it's easy to see why they are being included in personalized vows. Here are several examples.

Officiant (addressing the groom—referring to the child):

"And do you, _____, take _____ as your own, promising to love her and care for her, providing for her needs, physical, and spiritual?"

Groom:

"I do."

Officiant (addressing the child):

"And do you, _____, take _____, to be your loving father from this day forward?"

The child:

"I do."

Groom (addressing the child):

"_____, I place this ring on your finger as a sign of my loving promise made this day."

Note: The bride may recite these same vows to the groom's child, also placing a ring on the child's finger.

*****

"Because of you, my heart is at peace at last; because of you, I am happy and stable; because of you, I look forward to the future with joy instead of dread; because of you, my world is whole again; because of you, I believe in marriage anew; and because of you, my children will be blessed with a loving mother/father.

"You are the kindest, gentlest, most loving person I have ever met; what a blessing that I met you that day after church (personalize this to meet your circumstances) and that our friendship grew into a love that is eternal. I commit myself to you this day as your husband/wife and as the mother/father of your children. May God bless our marriage and our new family."

*****

"Not only do I vow to be a good and faithful husband to you, _____, but I also vow to be a patient, loving father to _____, _____, and _____, caring for them and providing for them as my own. I vow to be their strength and their emotional support, loving them with all my heart from this day forward."

*****

"As we become one on this, our wedding day, we become part of each other: your feelings become my feelings; your sorrows become my sorrows; your joys become my joys; your worries become my worries, and your children become my children.

"I promise to be a true and faithful husband/wife and father/mother, always there to comfort you, rejoice with you and endure all the complexities of life that we will face together as a family in the years to come. My love for you and the children is pure and unshakable and I hereby commit myself to all of you from this day forth and forevermore."

*****

Groom (addressing his bride):

"I love you, _____, and I love your children as my very own. My joy is multiplied tenfold because of _____ and _____. Their love fills a void in my life, a place that has remained empty for all of these years; filled now with their innocent sweetness and trusting devotion, I am complete at last.

And so, we are a family and I am blessed beyond belief as I marry you this day, my precious one, my Godsend. I vow to be a true and faithful husband/wife to you, in sickness or in health, in joy or in sorrow, in good times or in bad, from this day forward and forevermore, and I don't take my responsibilities as a father lightly, but with great gravity and sincerity. I vow to be a faithful, loving, tender and nurturing father/mother as well, always there for _____ and _____, not only providing their physical needs, but their emotional needs as well, always a good listener, a loving counselor, and a friend."

*****

"I have promised to love you and to be a faithful husband/wife, but I would like to add another vow, a promise to love _____ as my own child, to provide for him/her and to be a faithful father/mother, always concerned for his/her welfare, and his/her every need."

*****

"_____, did you know that you are a little bit of heaven to me? Although the golden days of childhood come and go so quickly, I promise that I will always be there for you. I love you dearly and I promise to be a faithful father to you for all the days of my life."

Vow to a New Step-Daughter

"_____, I love your Mommy, and today I have taken her as my wife; but, did you know that I love you dearly as well? I want to be as a father to you, and I invite you into my heart. We will have happy times together, you and your Mommy and I. And with this ring I give you my love." (Slides the ring onto the girl's finger.)

Vow to a New Step-Son

"_____, I love your Daddy, and today I have taken him as my husband; but, did you know that I love you dearly as well? I want to be as a mother to you, and I invite you into my heart. We will have happy times together, you and your Daddy and I. And with this ring I give you my love." (Slides the ring onto the boy's finger.)

Note: Instead of a ring, a new stepparent may present a bracelet or a necklace.

Include a Family Medallion or Circle of Acceptance Ceremony

See Chapter 21.

Include a Family Unity Candle Ceremony

A traditional unity candle ceremony consists of the lighting of a central candle from two separate candles held by the bride and groom, to symbolize the uniting of two lives into one.

A family unity candle ceremony is similar to the one previously described, except that there are additional candles—one for each child. So, the bride, groom, and each child lights the central candle at the same time, symbolizing they have formed a new family unit, unified as one.

A variation of this procedure is for the bride and her children to hold one candle, and the groom and his children to hold the other candle. These two candles are used to light the central candle at the same time.

Another poignant variation is for the bride and groom to light the central candle from their respective candles, then light their children's candles from the wick of the central candle.

Children Included in Congregational Blessing

Children are often included as part of the congregational blessing upon the bride, groom, and their child or children.

Minister (to the congregation):

"Will you lend your hearts and concerns to this couple and their children, upholding them in prayer and encouraging them in their new life together?"

The congregation responds:

"We will."

Chapter 37

NEW LIFE
CEREMONY

A New Life Ceremony, also known as a ceremony of love and renewal, is a poignant, touching wedding ceremony for those who have recovered from addictions, such as drug or alcohol addictions.

Every marriage ceremony is special in its own way, as the bride and groom give their hearts and lives to each other in wedded matrimony. A New Life Ceremony, however, is extra-special, if there can be such a thing. The reason for this is because, not only is the ceremony a celebration of the couple's love for each other, but also a celebration of their recovery.

A new life ceremony cries out to be personalized. Following is an example of a New Life Ceremony that has been personalized for the couple.

Convocation

Officiant:

"We have gathered here today to witness the marriage of _____ (bride) and _____ (groom). However, not only do we rejoice with them as they marry and embark on their life together as husband and wife, we also share their joy as they experience together the victory of new life through recovery and renewal. The victory they share is a gift they will treasure throughout all the years of their married life, a treasured gift for which they will give thanks, with tears of laughter and joy."

Invocation

Officiant:

"Thank you for bringing _____(bride) and _____(groom) together. Thank you for the love you have given them toward each other. May your love encircle them during this service, and may their marriage be richly filled with the love and joy only You can bring. Amen."

Reading

The bride's cousin reads the following from Ecclesiastes 4, verses 9 through 12:

"Two are better than one, because they have a good reward for their toil. For if they fall, one will lift up his fellow; but woe to him who is alone when he falls and has not another to lift him up. Again, if two lie together, they are warm; but how can one be warm alone? And though a man might prevail against one who is alone, two will withstand him."

Expression of Intent

Officiant to the bride:

"_____, is it your intent to marry _____ today? To bond to him as his wife?"

Bride: "Yes."

To the groom:

"_____, is it your intent to marry _____ today? To bond to her as her husband?"

Groom: "Yes."

Vows

Groom:

"_____ (bride), you are my healer, my comforter, and the joy of my life. Your love has restored my torn, broken heart; your smile has healed my pain; and your caring spirit has rescued mine from the dark places. May our love be always bright, always beautiful and always new. _____, I vow to be a faithful, loving husband, to care for you, to comfort you and to cherish you for as long as we both shall live."

Bride:

"_____ (groom), you are the sunshine of my life after the storms, my sweet nectar after the painful seasons of my days. I am proud to marry you this day and become your wife. Our lives have been touched by a very special love, as soft as the dawn, as radiant as the sun, and as beautiful as a rainbow that enfolds us after a storm. _____, I promise to be faithful to you, to honor you, to suffer with you, and to rejoice with you for as long as we both shall live."

Ring Exchange

Officiant:

"Now, may I have a token of your sincerity that you will keep these vows?"

(The best man gives the bride's ring to the officiant who holds it up and says:)

"This ring is a symbol of your vows and wearing it bears witness to your marital fidelity."

(The officiant hands the bride's ring to the groom and instructs him to place it on her finger.)

Officiant (to the groom):

"Do you, _____, give this ring to _____ as a token of your love and fidelity, and as a sign of the bond of new life and renewal?"

Groom: "I do."

(The officiant takes the groom's ring from the maid or matron of honor and gives it to the bride, instructing her to place it on her groom's finger.)

Officiant (to the bride):

"Do you, _____, give this ring to _____as a token of your love and fidelity, and as a sign of the bond of new life and renewal?"

Bride:

"I do."

Unity Candle Ceremony

(The bride and groom walk together to the unity candle.)

Officiant:

"_____ (bride) and _____ (groom), the two smaller candles symbolize your individual lives and families. Each of you now take one of the lighted candles and simultaneously light the unity candle, symbolizing that your individual lives and families are now joined in one light."

The bride and groom light the unity candle and then return to their place in front of the officiant.

Communal Candlelight Vows

Officiant (addressing the guests, who were each given unlighted candles as they entered the ceremony venue):

"You have just witnessed the marriage vows of _____ (bride) and _____ (groom). You have also witnessed the unity candle ceremony as they simultaneously lit the unity candle with the lighted wicks of their individual candles, representing the uniting of their individual lives as one."

(Addressing the guests):

"Please rise as you participate in the communal candlelight vows of support for this couple, pledging to love them, encourage them, and support them through all their years of married life."

(Addressing the bride and groom, as he lights a candle for each of them):

"_____ and _____ please use your lighted candles to light the candles of your family and friends."

(The bride and groom light the candles of the first guest sitting on their respective sides of the ceremony venue. These guests then turn to the next person, light his or her candle, and so on, until everyone in the venue holds a lighted candle.)

(Addressing the guests):

"Please raise your candles high and repeat these vows after me:

"We vow...

To support _____ and _____...

We will love them and encourage them...

Throughout all their years of their lives..."

(The officiant thanks the guests and asks them to extinguish their candles.)

Pronouncement of Marriage and the Kiss

Officiant:

"And now, by the power vested in me by the laws of the state of _____, I pronounce you husband and wife."

To the groom:

"You may kiss your bride."

Benediction

Officiant:

"Bless this couple as they go forth into their life together as husband and wife. May they give thanks each day to their higher power who has answered their prayers and given the gifts of love, renewal and new life. God grant them the serenity to accept the things they cannot change, the courage to change the things they can, and the wisdom to know the difference. Amen."

Chapter 38

NATURE
CEREMONY

Outdoor weddings have become popular for couples who want to escape the confines of a church, or any other manmade edifice. An outdoor wedding evokes a natural ambience, glorious and sacred as the bride and groom are married in "God's cathedral."

The ceremony may include any elements the bride and groom choose. However, they may wish to adopt one of these vow phrasings for their nature wedding:

Garden or Forest Ceremony

Bride/groom:

"As we stand in the shade of God's creation, I offer myself to you as your husband/wife. Our love is reflected in the flowers' blooms and the strength of the towering trees, always growing, always searching for perfection, just as the trees reach for the heavens and the blooms open their faces to the sun. Just as this garden/forest is a living thing, so may our union continue always to thrive until death do part us from his earth."

*****

Bride/groom:

"As we stand in this garden among these exquisite flowers, I offer you the flower of my heart as my wedding gift to you. This flower is pure and innocent; beautiful and eternal. It needs the care and nourishment that only you can give it. Place this flower within your own heart; love it; keep it safe; and give it light; and may it bloom forever from this day forward as I commit it to you with my eternal love as your wife/husband."

(The bride and groom may actually hand a flower to each other as he or she recites this vow.)

Outdoor Wedding in the Snow

Bride/groom:

"_____, I give myself to you this day, to be your husband/wife. I promise to love you with a love as pure and lovely as the snow, and a heart as warm as the radiant sun overhead. I promise to be true to you all the days of my life, with a loyalty and devotion as immense and seamless as the sky above."

Mountain Wedding

Groom:

"_____(bride), as we stand here in this magnificent setting, I vow to love you and be true to you as long as we both shall live. And as the trees stand tall and provide safety and shelter against the storm, I promise to provide for you and be your shelter for any storms we may face together."

Bride:

"_____(groom), I vow to love you and be true to you for as long as we both shall live. Just as these mountains are strong and enduring, so my love will always be for you."

Seaside Wedding

Bride/groom:

"As we stand beside the ocean tide, may our love always be as constant and unchanging as these waves that wash beneath our feet, flowing endlessly from the depths of the sea. Your love came softly upon my heart, just as the foam comes softly upon the sand. And just as there will never be a morning without the ocean's flow, so there will never be a day without my love for you. I pledge myself to you this day and I promise to be your faithful husband/wife, as unchanging and dependable as the tide; as these waters nourish the Earth and sustain life, may my constant love nourish and sustain you until the end of time."

*****

Groom:

"_____(bride), as we stand in this glorious place, surrounded by our friends and family, I take you to be my wife. I promise to love you with a love as deep and wide as this ocean, and I promise to stand beside you through good times and bad, through plenty and want, through sickness and health, as steady and dependable as these unceasing waves crashing against the sand."

Bride:

"_____ (groom), I take you to be my husband. I promise to love you with a love so immense and boundless that it can't be measured, just as no one can count the grains of sand on this beach. I promise to stand beside you through good times and bad, through plenty and want, through sickness sand health, as sure and steady as the flight of the seagulls soaring overhead."

*****

Bride/groom:

"As the sea is eternal, so is our love; as the wind is all-encompassing, so is our love; as the earth is solid beneath our feet, so is our love. And yet, our love is so great that it even soars beyond the sea and the wind and the Earth. It is so perfect to be standing beside you here, among these elements which reflect the love we have for each other. Every year on our anniversary, we will come here, to stand on this very spot, as we commit ourselves to each other anew, just as I commit myself to you this day."

Other Appropriate Additions

- ∞ Ceremony of the Wishing Stones, described in Chapter 23, which provides the wedding guests an opportunity to participate in a forest or seaside wedding. The guests are given, or may gather their own, stones or seashells, which are then placed in a container or thrown into the sea as the guests recite their wishes or blessings for the bride and groom.

- ∞ A Sand Ceremony, described in Chapter 25, is a meaningful addition to a seaside or waterside wedding.

- ∞ A rose ceremony, described in Chapter 22, which is especially poignant for a garden ceremony.

VIII.

THE BEFORE AND AFTER

Your wedding ceremony is the most important part of your day, and should be planned with great thought and care. Hopefully, by the time you've read this far, you have a sense of the decisions you'll need to make.

But what about the before and after? In the months and weeks leading up to your wedding day, your calendar will be filled with parties, planning, shopping, and coming up with the money to pay for it all. Then, after the ceremony, of course, will be your reception, your honeymoon, more parties, and all the fun stuff, such as writing thank-you notes.

In the next two chapters you'll find a brief description of the activities that will fill your before and after.

VIII

THE BEFORE-LIFE AFTER

Chapter 39

BEFORE THE CEREMONY

"The before" is filled with planning, parties, and to-do's. Here is a thumbnail sketch of what happens before your wedding day.

Announce Your Engagement

Your engagement may be announced during a formal dinner party or an informal family get-together. You may also announce your engagement in your local newspaper, with or without an engagement photo.

Plan Your Wedding Budget

You need to sit down with your parents, and anyone else who will be funding your wedding, to make a plan. If you don't set a budget before you start spending, the budget will plan you, and the next thing you know someone is putting a second mortgage on their home, or the credit cards are being charged to the max. You can plan a beautiful wedding on whatever funds you can raise. In fact, in my book, *How to Have a Big Wedding on a Small Budget, 4th edition*, I explain how it can be done.

Hire Your Service Providers

You'll need to hire your service providers as soon as possible after you have determined the amount of money you have to spend on your wedding. Here is a list of the most important service providers:

- Wedding planner or wedding day coordinator
- Printer (invitations, announcements, and so forth)
- Caterer
- Bakery
- Florist
- Tuxedo service
- Musicians
- Photographer
- Videographer
- Limousine service
- Wedding-day makeup artist
- Wedding-day hair stylist

Register for Gifts

Register for wedding gifts as soon as you become engaged, because the gift registry isn't only for your wedding guests, but for anyone attending an engagement party, bridal shower, or any other pre-wedding party. Think outside the box when it comes to registering for gifts. In addition to the standard registry at a department store, you can also register at a camping and mountaineering store, hardware store, garden supply store, furniture store, art gallery, mortgage company, or travel agency. That's right—you can even register for a down payment on a home, or for your honeymoon expenses!

Create the Wedding Guest List

Start on this project as soon as possible, asking each set of parents to make an A list and a B list. The A list contains the names of the must-invites, such as relatives and very close family friends. The B list contains the names of the would-like-to-invite-if-we-can-afford-it guests. The bride and groom should do the same. Then, if possible, everyone should get together at one time to go over the lists. Hopefully, you'll be able to invite everyone on your A lists and at least most on your B list.

Shop for Wedding Attire

This includes your bridal attire, plus the bridesmaids dresses, mothers' and grandmothers' dresses, and attire for the rest of your wedding party. The groom should also reserve tux rentals for himself and his attendants.

Purchase Gifts

The bride and groom have some gift-buying to do before the wedding. They should give thank-you gifts to their parents, members of their wedding party, and others who participate or help with the wedding. They may also decide to purchase personal wedding gifts for each other. (See my *Contemporary Guide to Wedding Etiquette* book for gift suggestions.)

Obtain the Marriage License

Call as soon as possible to obtain the requirements and procedure for obtaining your marriage license. In some instances, the county may require a waiting period between the date you obtain the license and the date of the wedding. Don't leave this until the last minute.

Pre-Marital Counseling

Your officiant may require premarital counseling, or you may decide to have it whether it is required or not. Meet with your priest, clergyman, rabbi, or other officiant or parish figure as soon as possible so that you know what is expected.

Plan the Honeymoon

The groom or the bride and groom together may plan their honeymoon. These plans should be made as soon as you've set your wedding date.

Attend Pre-Wedding Parties

The bride will be invited to bridal or co-ed showers, plus a bachelorette party, if there is one and may also attend or host a bridesmaids' luncheon a week or so before the wedding.

The groom will attend co-ed showers, if any are planned, plus his bachelor party, which, hopefully, will not be held the night before the wedding.

Write Toasts Ahead of Time

If you plan on toasting each other during the wedding reception, or offering toasts to family members in attendance, it's a good idea to write them ahead of time. Try to memorize them and practice delivering them out loud in front of a mirror. For toasting ideas, see my book, *Diane Warner's Complete Book of Wedding Toasts, 2nd edition*.

Rehearsal Dinner

This dinner is held immediately following the wedding rehearsal, which usually takes place the evening before the wedding. It is traditionally hosted by the groom's parents, although in today's world, anyone may host it: both sets of parents; any friends or relatives; or by the parents, the bride and groom, and anyone else who wants to help out. This meal may be formal or informal, held at the wedding site, in a restaurant, or in a private home.

Pre-Wedding Breakfast or Lunch

If the wedding is scheduled for late afternoon or evening, it's nice if someone hosts a light breakfast or luncheon for the couple's parents and members of the wedding party. This meal should be light, easy to fix, and easy to eat.

To read more about the before, pick up a copy of my book, *Diane Warner's Contemporary Guide to Etiquette*.

Chapter 40

AFTER THE CEREMONY

"The after" is filled with activities, beginning with your reception, and ending with the thank-you notes. Here's a thumbnail sketch of what to expect after the ceremony.

Your Wedding Reception

This is the most joyful celebration you'll ever attend. The ceremony is over—it was perfect in every way—and now it's time to celebrate with friends and family.

Afterglow

An afterglow is an intimate gathering that includes the bride and groom, their immediate families, and any close friends who came from out of town. This get-together follows the reception and is usually hosted by one of the bride's or groom's close relatives. It is usually held in a private home. A light meal is served. No planning on your part— all you need to do is glow for the guests.

Morning-After Breakfast or Brunch

This can be anything from a formal brunch at a resort, to an informal sausage-and-waffle breakfast in someone's home, usually the home of a close relative, friend, or neighbor. This is where you say your goodbyes before leaving on your honeymoon, if you didn't do so immediately after the reception or the afterglow.

Wedding Announcements Should be Mailed

Designate someone to be in charge of mailing your wedding announcements one or two days after the wedding. These announcements go to those who were not invited to the wedding, usually out-of-town friends and relatives, and will need to be addressed before the wedding.

Newspaper Announcement

Your wedding announcement should appear in your local newspaper soon after your wedding, unless you delay the announcement so that your wedding photo can be included. Prepare the wording for this announcement before the wedding.

After-the-Honeymoon Gift-Opening Party

The couple's parents often host this party, a casual evening where the bride and groom open their wedding gifts. Only immediate family members and a few close friends are invited.

Preservation of Your Bridal Gown

Your gown should be cleaned and stored as soon as possible after your wedding day. Take it to a dry cleaners that specializes in this type of cleaning.

Write the Thank-You Notes

Contrary to popular belief, you do not have a year to write your thank-you notes. Start on them as soon as you return from your honeymoon. Write three or four every day, with the goal to have them all mailed no later than six weeks after the wedding. It will help if you write as many thank-you notes as possible for gifts received and opened before the wedding.

To read more about the after, pick up a copy of my book, *Diane Warner's Contemporary Guide to Etiquette.*

Epilogue

It has been a joy to put this book together for you. I hope it helps you plan your very special wedding ceremony. Remember to personalize your ceremony as much as you possibly can so that it will be uniquely yours. When you look back on your ceremony in the years to come, I want your memories to be sweet.

Have a wonderful wedding!

Diane Warner

SAMPLE CEREMONY PROGRAM

Here are a few reasons why a ceremony program is important:

- It introduces the members of the wedding party and their relationship to the bride or groom.
- It gives the order of the service.
- It explains any unusual or creative elements of the ceremony. For example, the fact that the standing wreath of pink roses and baby's breath is in honor of a recently deceased family member; or the fact that the bride is wearing her mother's or grandmother's wedding gown or veil.
- It provides a way to thank those who helped with the wedding.
- It becomes a treasured memento of the ceremony, not only for the bride, groom, and their families, but for the guests as well.

A ceremony program can be professionally printed, along with your invitations, or it can be created on your home computer, using any cursive or fancy font, then printed onto parchment or fine linen paper. Once printed, it can be rolled into a scroll, tied with a ribbon, or folded and tied at the fold with a narrow satin ribbon. Typically, a program is printed on an 8 1/2 × 11-inch piece of paper that has been folded in half, resulting in four pages.

You can be as creative as you want with your content, including photos of you and your maid of honor when you were kids together; the love poem your fiancé wrote for you when he proposed; or the story of how your grandma's veil was lovingly preserved through the years.

To give you an idea of where to start, here is a sample ceremony program for you to use as a boilerplate:

Page One

Rachel and Joshua

November 10, 2007

Lakewood Community Church

Lakewood, Colorado

Page Two

Wedding Party

Parents of the Bride and Groom

Mr. and Mrs. Charles Emerson Thompson

Dr. and Mrs. Henry James Nelson

Maid of Honor	*Deanna Thompson*	*Sister of the Bride*
Best Man	*Donald Nelson*	*Brother of the Groom*
Bridesmaids	*Jill Johnson*	*Friend of the Bride*
	Helena Nelson	*Sister of the Groom*
	Ashley Fayton	*Sister of the Groom*

	Loni Halani	Friend of the Bride
Groomsmen	Randy Jefferson	Friend of the Groom
	Gerald Nelson	Brother of the Groom
	James Thompson	Brother-in-law of the Groom
	James Henderson	Friend of the Groom
Flower Girls	Madison Thompson	Niece of the Groom
	Michelle Thompson	Niece of the Groom
Ring Bearer	Jaime Nelson	Nephew of the Groom
Candle-lighters	Darla Castro	Friend of the Bride
	Linda Trump	Friend of the Bride and Groom
Officiants	Dr. Mitch Barton	Senior Pastor of Lakewood Community Church
	Rev. Eugene Johns	Uncle of the Bride
Organist	Rosalie Myers	Friend of the Bride
Soloist	Thomas Page	Friend of the Groom
Flautist	Laura Tipton	Friend of the Bride

Page Three

Order of Service

Prelude	"To God Be the Glory," performed by Laura Tipton
Candle-lighting	"Jesu, Joy of Man's Desiring"
Seating of Honored Guests	"The Wedding Song," sung by Thomas Page

Lighting of the Memorial Candle and Seating of Mother of the Bride

Processional   "Trumpet Voluntary"

Giving of the Bride

Prayer

Scripture Reading

Pastoral Comments

Exchanging of Vows and Rings

Lighting of Unity Candle

Pronouncement of Marriage

Introduction of the Bride and Groom

Jumping of the Broom

Recessional   "Wedding March" from The Sound of Music

Reception to follow in Lavinda Rose Garden

Page Four

The Memorial Candle is in loving memory of Naomi
Chambers, grandmother of the bride.

The Unity Candle symbolizes the unity of the bride and
groom as they leave their families and become one.

The Jumping of the Broom is an African-American wedding
tradition that demonstrates the sweeping away of the old life and
the starting of a new life of commitment to each other.

Special Thanks to ...

The Classic Car Club of Lakewood for providing and
decorating our getaway car!

Susan Heston for her loving efforts coordinating our wedding.

INDEX

ABOUT THE AUTHOR

Diane Warner is the best-selling author of 22 books, including *Complete Book of Wedding Vows*, *Big Weddings on a Small Budget*, *Complete Book of Wedding Showers*, and *Complete Book of Wedding Toasts*. She also writes for magazines and newspapers, such as *Boston Line*, *New York Daily News*, *Washington Weddings*, and *BJ's Journal*, plus Websites, including *dreamweavers.com* and *theweddingshow.net*. She speaks professionally, conducts seminars, and is a frequent guest on radio talk shows, as well as national TV, including CNN, HGTV, and the Discovery Channel.

Diane attended UCLA on a theatre arts scholarship and is past member and officer with NSA (National Speakers Association). She lives with her husband, Jack, in Tuscon, Arizona. They have two grown children, four grandchildren, and enjoy playing golf and singing in a touring choir sponsored by their church. Visit Diane at her Website, *dianewarnerbooks.com*.

Other Books by Diane Warner

Published by John Wiley Publishing

Single Parenting for Dummies, co-authored with Marion
Peterson

Published by F & W Publications, Betterway Books

How to Have a Big Wedding on a Small Budget, 4th edition
Big Wedding on a Small Budget Planner and Organizer
How to Have a Fabulous, Romantic Honeymoon on a Budget
Beautiful Wedding Decorations and Gifts on a Small Budget
Picture-Perfect, Worry Free Weddings
How to Have a Great Retirement on a Limited Budget

Published by Career Press, Inc. / New Page Books

Contemporary Guide to Wedding Etiquette
Best Wedding Ever
Complete Book of Wedding Toasts, 2nd edition
Complete Book of Wedding Vows, 2nd edition
Complete Book of Wedding Showers
Complete Book of Baby Showers

Diane Warner's Wedding Question & Answer Book
Diane Warner's Big Book of Parties
Diane Warner's Complete Book of Children's Parties
Diane Warner's Great Parties on Small Budgets

Published by Pentan Overseas, Inc. (Books on Tape)
The Perfect Wedding Planner

Published by JIST Works, Inc.
(co-authored with her husband, Jack, and Clyde Bryan)
The Unauthorized Teacher's Survival Guide, 3rd Edition
The Inside Secrets of Finding a Teaching Job, 3rd Edition

Published by Accent Books, David C. Cook Publishing
Puppets Help Teach
Puppet Scripts for Busy Teachers